FRI FLYT

©2012 Fri Flyt AS
Original title: Opplev Sunnmørsalpane (Fri Flyt 2011)
Translation: Howard John Medland
Graphic design: Eva Camilla Brandt
Front cover photo: Arnfinn Tønnesen
Back cover photo: André Spica
Paper: 130g Galerie Art Silk
Typeset: Whitman 10/13
Image processing: Eirik Vaage and Torgeir Haugaard
Print: Interface Media AS
Maps: Kartagena AS, permission NE16662-161111

Fri Flyt AS
Mølleparken 6
0459 Oslo

Phone: +47 22 04 46 00
Web: www.friflyt.no

ISBN: 978-82-93090-06-9

Stig J. Helset, Fredrik Sigurdh and Eirik Vaage

THE SUNNMØRE ALPS
An Outdoor Guide

View north down Hjørundfjorden from Kårdalstindane. Bjørke bottom left.
Utolhornet opposite. Jakta to the right. Photo: Håvard Myklebust

CONTENTS

On the way towards Brekketindane. Slogen in the background. Photo: Ståle Johan Aklestad

2.1 THE COAST

Out on the coast lies Ålesund, the largest town in
the region. Known as the Venice of the North, it
has about 50 000 inhabitants. It is a fantastic Art
Noveau town, and from the highest local vantage
point Fjellstua there is a magnificent view, not just
of the town, but also of the Sunnmøre Alps and
the Atlantic Ocean. Other important towns on the
coast are Ulsteinvik and Fosnavåg. The western
reaches of Sunnmøre are barren and exposed.
The fauna and flora are reminiscent of the coastal
areas of the Faeroes, Iceland and Scotland. Out
here the wind blows hard across the skerries and
rocks, with little to stand in the way of the forces
of nature. In these outer regions there are few
peak climbs over 600 metres, and rarely enough
snow to go skiing. On the other hand, the area is
an eldorado for a variety of water activities: diving,
kayak paddling, kiting and surfing are obvious
choices out here where the horizon stretches to
infinity. In addition the area offers high quality
cragging and bouldering. Not surprisingly, the
weather is a regular topic of conversation among
the locals. The lighthouse keepers on the remote
island of Svinøya have experienced winds of up to
120 knots and gigantic waves that have reached
the top of the lighthouse over 40 metres above the
water.

Sunset over Runde lighthouse. Photo: Arnfinn Tønnesen

Climbing on Bladet, Molladalen. Photo: Arnfinn Tønnesen

2.2   KOLÅS- AND RÅNAHALVØYA

In the central part of the Sunnmøre Alps you will find the small towns of Ørsta, Volda, Stranda and Sykkylven, all surrounded by a characteristically alpine landscape of spectacular high mountains, through which the three fjords Dalsfjorden, Austefjorden and Hjørundfjorden cut their way. At an angle to these fjords are new valleys and hanging valleys below the majestic peaks that dive 1000-1600 metres perpendicularly down to the water's edge. If you mix Lofoten, a little of Alaska's fjord landscape and a taste of south-western New Zealand, you will get an idea of what the fjord and mountain landscape of Sunnmøre has to offer. Some of the finest experiences are to be had in the mountains around Molladalen, Ørsta town centre, Standalhytta and Patchellhytta. Molladalen offers climbing from two to six pitches in all grades in the summer. In winter these mountains offer exciting gully skiing. In early winter, however, it is the mountains right above Ørsta that are the most popular for skiing. Just a couple of hours' walk from the car you will find descents to suit every taste and at all levels of difficulty. A little later in the winter it is the area round Standalhytta that is most popular, with ski trips in magnificent surroundings to peaks like Kolåstinden, Sætretindane, Standalhornet and many more. Patchellhytta above Hotel Union in Øye is the starting point for the wettest dreams a skier can dream: Slogen, Smørskredtindane and Brekketindane. Most of these peaks were first scaled by overseas pioneers like Slingsby, Patchell, Oppenheim and Arbuthnot in the late 1800s and early 1900s. These were the aristocrats of their time who saw how unique the Sunnmøre Alps were long before the locals realised what was right outside their front door, and we hope and believe that a new generation of outdoor enthusiasts recognise the value of this well preserved treasure. In addition to these famous mountains, today's trailblazing generation can experience mountain biking, kayaking, surfing, climbing, sport climbing, bouldering, and much more fun besides, in the great outdoors that is Sunnmøre.

2.3　TAFJORDFJELLA

The eastern, inner part of Sunnmøre is reached by following the commanding Storfjord in from the coast, ending with the world-famous Geirangerfjord as its grand finale. Surrounding the ends of the fjords you find Tafjordfjella, and at the foot of these mountains lie a number of well-known tourist destinations such as Geiranger, Valldal, Tafjord, Norddal with renowned passes and vantage points like Trollstigen, Ørnesvingane and Dalsnibba. In extent Tafjordfjella is the largest area in Sunnmøre for hiking, and offers many fine peaks, with Puttegga as the highest at 1999 metres. The mountains here are generally higher than on Kolås- and Rånahalvøya, but they are also less alpine in form. This is Ålesund - Sunnmøre Tourist Association's (ÅST) playground, and they run a number of mountain lodges and cabins that provide overnight accommodation for the DNT (Norwegian Trekking Association). Two of the lodges also serve meals during the summer. It is common practice to hike from cabin to cabin in this area, which has waymarked trails in the summer. In winter there is little traffic here, and navigation is also more demanding. But at Easter ÅST usually mark the trails between the various cabins in the area. Alpine ski touring is also very popular here, especially after the Trollstigen mountain pass has been opened for traffic in May.

Valldal and the surrounding area is also interesting for a number of other activities, such as rafting, paddling, downhill biking, longboarding, canyoning and climbing. The climate is drier in these inner regions than out on the coast, and summer temperatures can be high. Valldal is also famous for its tasty fruit, and the village boasts its own Strawberry Fair.

Ready for a walk in Taljordfjella. Photo: Kristin Oftedal Vinje

Skiing down Brekketindane. Slogen in the background. Photo: Eirik Vaage

3 ALPINE SKI TOURING

Alpine ski touring is perhaps the one outdoor activity in Sunnmøre that attracts most participants – both locals and visitors – which is not really surprising, given the fact that the Sunnmøre Alps offer an unusually broad range of peaks to suit every taste. The short distances from small towns and hamlets to the foot of the mountains mean that you are soon on the spot, and the ski trips vary immensely – from the very short and simple to the longer, steeper and more demanding. The first ski tourists came up the Hjørundfjord from Ålesund by boat at the turn of the 20th century to enjoy the mountains surrounding Standaleidet. After Ålesund Skiing Club was established in 1908, there was a real boom in ski tourism, and when the first skiing competition was organised in Fingersida in 1909, there were over 200 skiers onboard the steamboat from Ålesund. The same winter witnessed the first known ascent on skis of Kolåstinden. In the decade after the war the interest in skiing spread from the upper classes in the town to other classes in the local population, and many peaks were visited by skiers during this period. But right up until the end of the last century it was most common to go skiing in the spring, even though some of the keenest skiers and climbers also attacked summits in winter. In the mid-1990s this pattern changed, as more and more local and visiting ski enthusiasts started to explore steeper mountain slopes throughout the winter, i.e. from the first snowfall, which is usually in October/November, until the last of the spring snow, which normally lasts until the end of June. All the estimates in this chapter regarding time apply to the ascent only, and they are of course approximate. Enjoy your ski trip in Sunnmøre's powder snow, but beware of the risk of avalanches, which is often considerable in the changeable climate of western Norway.

ROUTE OUTLINES

In the photo topos we have sketched in route outlines. A solid red line shows the normal route up the mountain. This line usually also indicates the normal route back down from the summit. In some of the photo topos we have in addition sketched in one or more dotted lines, which indicate other alternative, often extreme, descent routes. On many of the mountains you can also choose other descent routes than those illustrated in the overview photos.

Fun on skis just below the summit of Saudehornet. Photo: Stig J. Helset

From the left we see Nivane, Vardehornet, Saudehornet and Vallahornet.
Photo: Eirik Vaage

3.1   SAUDEHORNET (1303 m)

FROM THE PUMP HOUSE ABOVE ØRSTA TOWN CENTRE

This trip is popular throughout the winter and spring, because the mountain is easily accessible from the town centre, and the normal descent is very direct and spectacular. However, the route is often subject to avalanches.

Time: 3 hours.

Distance: 3-4 km.

Vertical ascent: 1150 m from the Pump House.

Equipment: Helmet, shovel, probe, transceiver, alpine touring or telemark skis and winter clothing. In hard snow you will need crampons and/or an ice axe to climb the final 200 vertical metres from Knekken and along the south ridge to the summit.

Hazards: General risk of avalanches on west side of Vikeskåla and extreme danger in all the steep gullies on Saudehornet. Danger of slip-sliding on hard snow. The cornice along the top ridge can be fairly large, so care is needed to avoid going too close to the edge here. Possible crevices in the gullies from the top ridge down towards Vikeskåla and Skytjådalen.

Approach: Turn off the E39 in the centre of Ørsta and follow Vikegeila straight up until you come to the Pump House and a large parking area. In winter it can be icy and difficult to drive all the way up the steep slope to the Pump House without a 4WD. In that case, park closer to the town centre and walk the last few hundred metres to the Pump House. From the steel gate follow the gravel road on foot or skis up to the third of the small pump houses. Traverse diagonally towards the Vikeelva, cross this river and aim for the lowest point on the ridge between Vallahornet and Saudehornet. Then follow the south ridge all the way to the summit, possibly having to carry your skis the final 200 vertical metres.

Descent: The usual descent is the same way as you came up, but then keep to the skier's right-hand side of the gully. The incline here is a steady 37 degrees for 600 wonderful metres, then gentler terrain back down to the river and the Pump House. On days safe from avalanches Saudehornet also offers more extreme descents for the experienced skier. If you follow the ridge westwards from the summit, you come to the top of two-three great gullies that dive down towards Vikeskåla. Here the incline can reach over 45 degrees. If you follow the ridge a couple of hundred metres in the other direction, eastwards, you arrive at the top of two even steeper and more spectacular gullies that run straight down to Skytjådalen, 800 metres below. From there you can ski down past Vallahornet and continue to the right. Turn sharp right at the power lines and follow these back to the river and the Pump House. Alternatively you can turn off towards the ridge between Vallahornet and Saudehornet when you have left the gullies themselves and follow the normal route down to the Pump House from there. We emphasize that these are routes that must be taken on days with absolutely no danger of avalanches and only by very experienced skiers.

Powder run down Vardehornet. Saudehornet in the background. Photo: Eirik Vaage

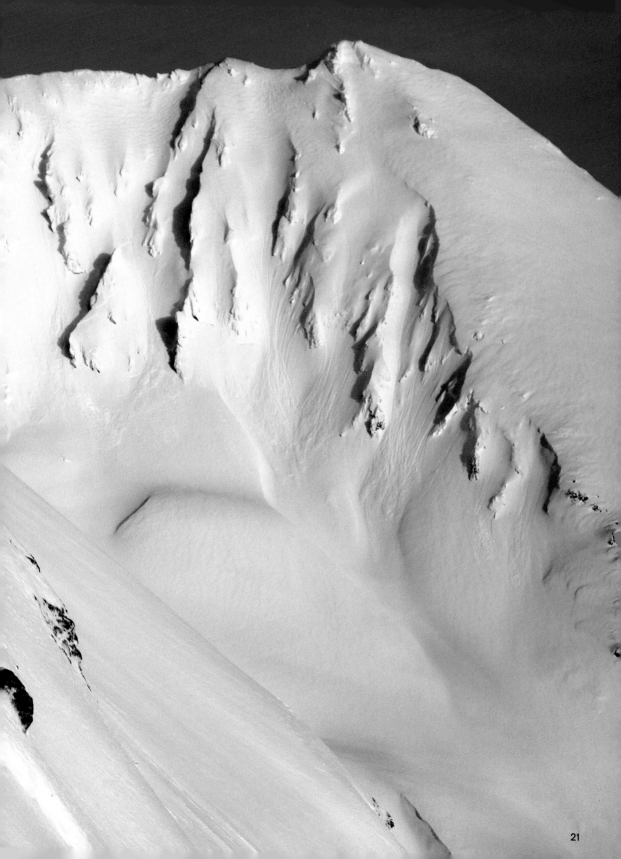

On the way down from Nivane. Ørsta town centre in the background.
Photo: Rikard Andreasson

3.2   NIVANE (936 m) / VARDEHORNET (1009 m)

FROM THE PUMP HOUSE ABOVE ØRSTA TOWN CENTRE

Nivane is easily accessible and offers excellent fast descents, often in powder snow in early winter.

Time:	2 hours.
Distance:	3 kilometres.
Vertical ascent:	800/850 m from the Pump House.
Equipment:	Helmet, shovel, probe, transceiver, alpine touring or telemark skis and winter clothing.
Hazards:	General risk of avalanches on south slopes of Nivane and west slope of Vikeskåla and high risk in the steep gullies on Vardehornet. Cornices on the top plateau from Nivane to Vardehornet.
Ascent:	The route to the Pump House is described under Saudehornet. From the steel gate follow the gravel road on foot or skis up to the third of the small pump houses. Turn northwest and aim for the ridge on Nivane. Follow this by tacking all the way up to the top cairn, which is at the back of the plateau. From there it is a gentle ascent northeast across the top plateau towards the summit of Vardehornet.
Descent:	From Nivane it is safest to descend the same way as you went up, along the ridge. But on days with no danger of avalanches you can ski more directly down the south slope with superb views of the Ørstafjord. This is a wonderful broad slope of up to 35 degrees which offers wide turns and high speeds on powder days. Remember to turn off back towards the third pump house before you reach the woods. From the top of Vardehornet there are two or three great ridges and gullies with a 40-45 degree incline down towards Vikeskåla. The area surrounding Saudehornet and Vardehornet is the arena for the annual X-Tind ski competition (ski alpinism) and X-Free (freeride), which attracts the best skiers in the country.

3.3 FINGEREN (1180 m)

FROM STANDALHYTTA

Fingeren can be reached comfortably during a morning in winter sunshine, and the descent is fantastic in powder snow.

Time: 2 hours.
Distance: 3 kilometres.
Vertical ascent: 780 m.
Equipment: Helmet, shovel, probe, transceiver, alpine touring or telemark skis and winter clothing. Normally, crampons, an ice axe and some safety equipment are needed to climb the final metres from the ridge to the summit.
Hazards: Risk of avalanches below Noklane at 700-800 metres.
Ascent: Head west from Standalhytta a short distance before you swing up past some crags. From here the route is pretty obvious up to a height of 800m, where you again veer west towards the ridge north of Fingeren. Snow conditions and your own skills and experience will decide whether you climb all the way up to the summit.
Descent: Go down the same way as you came up. Moderate descent with a 30 degree incline at its steepest.

Fingeren on the left, Kolåstinden in the centre and Sætretindane to the right.
Photo: Eirik Vaage

On the way towards Fingeren. Photo: Sindre Dimmen

On both sides of Standaleidet there is a whole range of great peaks for skiing, offering both moderate and extreme descents. At the same time this area offers a variety of accommodation for visitors, with the Standalhytta cabin as the most legendary among skiers. To reach it you take the RV655 from the town centre of Ørsta in the direction of Sæbø. After about 4 km, do not cross the bridge at Høgebrua, but drive straight on for about 7 km up the Follestaddal valley towards Kolåsen. From Kolåsen follow the gravel road (open all year) for about 4 km up onto Standalseidet.

3.4 KOLÅSTINDEN (1432 m)
FROM STANDALHYTTA

Kolåstinden is «The King of the Sunnmøre Alps», mainly due to its majestic appearance, but also because it offers a great skiing trip in moderate, but varied terrain.

Time: 3 hours.
Distance: 4 kilometres.
Vertical ascent: 1040 m.
Equipment: Helmet, shovel, probe, transceiver, alpine touring or telemark skis and winter clothing.
Hazards: Risk of avalanches as you enter the Kvanndal valley and risk of slip-sliding in Stretet and on the final incline before the summit. Beware also of possible crevasses in the glacier, especially below the top and during direct descents across the glacier.
Ascent: From Standalhytta or from the cabins just east of there, head in the direction of Fossane below Søre Sætretind. From the top of Fossane you follow a distinct V-shaped valley until you reach the open floor of Kvanndal valley itself. Veer north up to Appelsinhaugen, which is a resting stone at a height of 950m. Then head west-southwest and climb the steep flank up towards and through Stretet, which is a narrow passage in the ridge. Once safely past Stretet, you follow the edge of the glacier just below the ridge in the direction of the summit, which is now clearly visible all the way. Remove your skis if you feel it is too steep below the peak and climb the final metres on foot.
Descent: Most people go down the same way as they came up, and here the incline is rarely over 25 degrees. It is also fully possible to ski down into Kvanndalen via the glacier. But here the steepness increases dramatically towards the end, especially if you have not discovered the best line on the way up. In addition, there is a danger of falling into crevasses if you are not familiar with the conditions.

Skiing down the lower part of the Kolåsbreen glacier.
Photo: Håvard Myklebust

3.5 NORDRE SÆTRETIND (1365 m)
FROM STANDALHYTTA

Nordre Sætretind is most famous for its incredible gullies that offer really challenging runs in good conditions.

Time:	3 hours.
Distance:	4 km.
Vertical ascent:	970 m.
Equipment:	Helmet, shovel, probe, transceiver, alpine touring or telemark skis and winter clothing. On hard snow you will need crampons and/or an ice axe to climb the final 20 vertical metres from the cleft and up the gully to the summit.
Hazards:	Risk of avalanches as you enter the Kvanndal valley and risk of both avalanches and slip-sliding in the gully up from the valley. Extreme danger of avalanches and of slip-sliding in the steep gullies described in the descent.
Ascent:	From Standalhytta or from the cabins just east of there, head in the direction of Fossane below Søre Sætretind. From the top of Fossane you follow a distinct V-shaped valley until you reach the open stretch of land in Kvanndalen itself. Veer north towards the plain below Appelsinhaugen, and go diagonally eastwards in towards the gully at the far end of the valley. Go up the steep gully, if you prefer with your skis on your backpack. From the top of the gully you cross a flat area until you come to a broad ridge that leads up to a col just below the summit. Leave your skis in or below the col and follow a short gully to the left the last twenty vertical metres to the top.
Descent:	Nordre Sætretind has many great alternatives for the descent. The most moderate one heads east and down towards Fladalen. Follow that valley as far as the edge above Standalsætra. From here you can follow the works road in open deciduous woodland down to the road across Standaleidet. Follow the road on foot for one kilometre back to the car park at Standalhytta. Another alternative is to return the same way as you went up. The incline is over 40 degrees in the steepest parts of the gully that leads back down to Kvanndalen. There are also two-three extremely demanding descents in the even steeper gullies that cut through the ridge that runs from the top of the said gully and up to the summit. Here the incline can approach as much as 50 degrees. We emphasize that these are routes that must only be attempted on days that are 100% safe from avalanches with no risk of slip-sliding and then only by very experienced skiers.

A powder line in the evening sun on Nordre Sætretinden. Romedalstinden in the background. Photo Eirik Vaage

Winter climbing on Sætretindane. Photo: Åsmund Vaage

3.6 RANDERS' TOPP (1414 m)

FROM ÅRSNESET

The trip to Randers' topp is perhaps the most varied and impressive of all the classic spring ski trips in the Sunnmøre Alps.

Time: 4 hours.
Distance: 3 km if you go straight up the Årsnes glacier, 4 km via Ytstenesdalen.
Vertical ascent: 1400 m from the avalanche shed.
Equipment: Helmet, shovel, probe, transceiver, alpine touring or telemark skis and winter clothing. On hard snow you will need crampons and/or an ice axe to reach the summit of Randers' topp. If you also wish to conquer Mohns topp or climb on Bladet, you will need ropes, harness and safety equipment.
Hazards: The Årsnesfonna avalanche/snowdrift can be very large and can sweep right down to the fjord, at the same time as it is difficult to estimate when it will break. Do ask the locals for advice. There may also be a risk of avalanches up the steep slope from Ytstenesdalen towards the Årsnesbreen, if you choose that route. Note also that there may well be a crevasse at about 1150 metres on the glacier, and that there is usually a fairly large cornice on the top. The steep gullies from Mohns topp down towards Giganten and Molladalen can only be attempted in good snow on days with no risk of avalanches.
Approach: From Ålesund take the ferry Solavågen-Festøya. Follow the road south on the western shore of the Hjørundfjord in the direction of Standal. From Volda/Ørsta you can take the road over Standaleidet and follow the road north on the western shore of the Hjørundfjord. Stop at the avalanche shed at Årsneset. Early in the year you can put your skis on right down by the water's edge. Later in the year you must carry your skis on your sac part of the way up the hillside. You can choose the approach via the magnificent Ytstenesdalen or head straight up the Årsnesbreen. After you have reached the top of this glacier, there remains a short but steep snow slope up to the summit of Randers' topp. After you have been on the summit, you can ski back down the slope and head diagonally across towards Mohns topp. To climb up here safety gear is essential. Finally you can pay a visit to Bladet – a pinnacle that towers twenty metres above the glacier, and which is the unmistakable logo for Molladalen and the Sunnmøre Alps. The climbing is easy (grade 4), but the pointed summit is airy.
Descent: The upper section of Randers' topp has an incline of roughly 40 degrees, but down across the Årsnes glacier the terrain becomes less steep and more undulating. On the other hand, in optimum snow conditions you have the opportunity to ski all the 1414 metres straight down to the waterline, with a view of the Hjørundfjord and the mountains east of it all the way down. There are also steeper descents. From immediately below Mohns topp there is a steep gully down towards Ytstenesdalen. On the way you pass the majestic rock pinnacle Giganten, which stretches 50 metres straight up from the gully. Just as you pass Giganten, you must be on your guard, because you might have to climb past some cliffs. Another alternative that is excellent in good snow conditions is the Mohnsrenna gully,

View from Randers' topp. Photo: Håvard Myklebust

which dives at 45 degrees down towards Molladalen itself. The disadvantage of this choice of route is that you need access to transport when you come down to Melbøsætra summer pasture up the valley from Barstadvika and Festøya.

Two possible routes up and down from Randers' topp. Photo: Helge Standal

Descent from Randers' topp. Hjørundfjorden way down below.
Photo: Håvard Myklebust

Dropping just below the summit of Søre Grøtdalstind. Photo: Nina Gudevang

3.7 SØRE GRØTDALSTIND (1331 m)
FROM THE RV655 IN BONDALEN

This mountain has many visitors throughout the winter because of its accessibility, wonderful views and great descent.

Time:	3-4 hours.
Distance:	4 km.
Vertical ascent:	1230 m from Frøland.
Equipment:	Helmet, shovel, probe, transceiver, alpine touring or telemark skis and winter clothing. On hard snow you will need crampons and/or an ice axe to climb the final hundred metres from Himmelporten and up the gully/ridge to the summit.
Hazards:	General risk of avalanches on the south side of the mountain and especially in the gully from Himmelporten towards the summit. In the gully there is also a risk of slip-sliding on hard snow. Be aware of the possibility of a top cornice.
Approach:	Take the RV655 from the centre of Ørsta towards Sæbø. Turn left at the bridge with the sign to Kvistad about 3 km west of Sæbø. Park the car at Ner-Frøland or beside the new forestry road that runs for about 1 kilometre to Heimsætra summer pasture, before you head north towards the south side of Grøtdalstindane. Seasonal variations and snow conditions determine when you can put on your skis. Follow the most suitable route according to the conditions up the south side/south ridge, via gentler terrain and in towards the southwest ridge. Go through Himmelporten, which is a col about 100 metres below the summit, and follow the gully or ridge to the southern summit of Grøtdalstindane.
Descent:	The usual route back down is the same way as you went up. In good snow conditions it is possible to ski right from the summit. The incline approaches 40 degrees in the steepest sections near the top and on the south ridge.

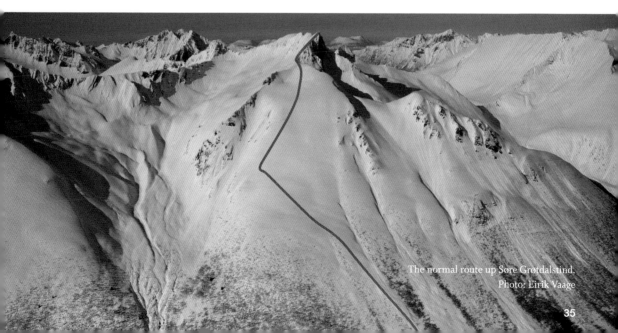

The normal route up Søre Grøtdalstind.
Photo: Eirik Vaage

3.8 SKÅRASALEN (1542 m)
FROM THE RV655 IN BONDALEN OR FROM KVISTADSÆTRA

Skårasalen is one of the most popular of all the ski mountains in Sunnmøre. Because of a long farm road that is closed to traffic in winter, this trip is usually made late in the autumn or ideally during the spring, when the road to Kvistadsætra has been opened.

Time: 3-4 hours from Kvistad, 2-3 hours from Kvistadsætra.

Distance: 7 km from Kvistad, 3 km from Kvistadsætra.

Vertical ascent: 1440 m from Kvistad, 1050 m from Kvistadsætra.

Equipment: Helmet, shovel, probe, transceiver, alpine touring or telemark skis and winter clothing.

Hazards: Normally one or more large avalanches will follow the gullies from the summit and down towards the car park at the end of the farm road at some time during the winter. Avoid tracking too far east on the top plateau/ridge, where there are often cornices.

Approach: Take the RV655 from the centre of Ørsta towards Sæbø. Turn right at the bridge with the sign to Kvistad about 3 km west of Sæbø, and drive about one kilometre along a gravel road as far as the barrier above the Kvistad farms. Snow conditions determine whether you must walk the 4 km from here to Kvistadsætra or whether you can drive all the way. From the car park at the seter there is 500 metre-long dirt track along the edge of arable land. Follow the track almost to the end, before turning left along a solid well marked footpath through open deciduous woodland. When you leave the woods, you can either follow the avalanche path in the gully that runs down from the top or climb the steep slope north of this gully to avoid the possible risk of avalanches. At 800 metres, head north into a marked snow valley. Climb this gently rising snow valley and eventually head eastwards until you have almost reached the col to Lisje-Skåradalen. From here you can follow a gentle ridge up towards the top plateau, which ends in a slight incline before the summit cairns. The trip from Kvistadsætra to the summit is moderate.

Descent: The usual route back down is the same way as you went up, possibly more directly down towards the snow valley after the top plateau. This descent is moderate, with the incline generally below 30 degrees. But Skårasalen offers other descents. The most extraordinary one runs from the summit and down to Skår via Lisje-Skåradalen. Turn off in the col and ski down the middle of the valley down a 25 degree incline. Here you have fantastic views of the Hjørundfjord and Slogen the whole way down to Skår. Snow conditions determine how far you can ski before you have to walk the rest of the way along a narrow sheep track to the ferry quay at Skår. Before starting the daytrip, remember to ring the ferry operator Fjord1 and ask the ferry to schedule a stop! Another and more extreme alternative goes right from the top and straight down the gullies towards Kvistadsætra. First ski down from the summit cairns and a couple of hundred metres across the top plateau. Then turn sharp left and attack the system of gullies with an incline of up to 45 degrees that leads you straight back to where you started the trip. Have fun, but beware of avalanches, sliding and precipices!

Rhythmic curves down the main ridge on Skårasalen. Photo: Knut Hustad

The normal route up Skårasalen. Photo: Eirik Vaage

ALPINE SKI TOURING STARTING FROM PATCHELLHYTTA IN HABOSTADDALEN

Patchellhytta is surrounded by some of the most spectacular and well-known mountains in the Sunnmøre Alps. Once you are installed at the cabin, these peaks are easily accessible for experienced alpinists. You can reach the cabin from three different approaches. The gentlest, but longest goes up Habostad valley from Stranda, and the route is obvious. The shortest, but without a doubt the steepest route goes up the hillside from the farms in Norangsdalen at Skylstad, which lies a couple of kilometres east of the famous Hotel Union at Øye. Follow the RV655 from Ørsta town centre to Sæbø. Take the ferry Sæbø-Lekneset and drive on for another 12 kilometres on the RV655 until you come to Skylstad. Cross the field over a bridge from the Skylstad farms and head slightly to the right after the bridge. Now follow a steep but good path up the hillside to the left of the large river. Keep on the path up to 600-700 metres, before aiming diagonally towards the pass between Slogen and Smørskedtindane, and continue a gentle climb up to the cabin (see sketch below). A route somewhere between these two extremes starts from Urke. Follow the RV655 from Ørsta town centre to Sæbø. Take the ferry Sæbø-Lekneset and drive on for another 2 kilometres on the RV655 until you come to Urke. Follow the signpost to Urkedalen from the RV655. Park at the power station above Haukåssætra, or further down the valley if the road is blocked by snow. Follow the marked path north of the watercourse until you reach the snow. Keep a little west of the floor of the gentle Langsæter valley. Climb up onto Steinreset, and ski down to the cabin in Habostaddalen. The trip takes about two hours from the power station.

Slogen to the left, Brekketindane behind and Smørskredtindane to the right. Skylstadbrekka in the foreground and Patchellhytta in the middle of the hanging valley. Photo: Eirik Vaage

A steep descent from the col below Store Brekketind. Photo: Eirik Vaage

The view from Slogen. Norangsfjorden way down below. Photo: Arnfinn Tønnesen

3.9 SLOGEN (1564 m)

FROM PATCHELLHYTTA

Slogen is probably the most famous peak in the whole of the Sunnmøre Alps and offers great descents.

Time: 2 hours.
Distance: 3 km.
Vertical ascent: 750 m.
Equipment: Helmet, shovel, probe, transceiver, alpine touring or telemark skis and winter clothing. On hard snow you will need crampons and/or an ice axe to climb the final 100-200 vertical metres to the summit.
Hazards: Risk of avalanches and slip-sliding during the descent from the top ridge and almost the whole way down.
Ascent: Ski from the cabin to Steinreset and follow the ridge that leads up to Slogen. Follow the ridge all the way to the summit. The ridge gradually becomes steeper, and snow conditions and your experience/skills must decide when you will tie your skis to your sac. If the snow is hard, you will need crampons and/or an ice axe on the final ascent up the ridge.
Descent: In good snow conditions Slogen offers fantastic descents right from the top. The incline is about 45 degrees from the top and down past the steepest crags. There is an extremely steep line towards the north, while the normal route straight down towards Steinreset and the cabin is a little less steep, especially after you have skied part of the way down. In this way it is possible to adapt the start of the descent to suit the snow conditions and your own skills.

On the way up Slogen. Photo: Rikard Andreasson

3.10 STORE SMØRSKREDTIND (1631 m)

FROM PATCHELLHYTTA

Store Smørskredtind offers what is probably the most extreme skiing line in the whole of the Sunnmøre Alps.

Time:	3 hours.
Distance:	3 km.
Vertical ascent:	800 m.
Equipment:	Helmet, shovel, probe, transceiver, alpine touring or telemark skis and winter clothing. On hard snow you will need crampons and/or an ice axe to climb the final 300 vertical metres up the gully to the summit.
Hazards:	Risk of avalanches in the whole area. Especially dangerous up towards the cleft on the north side, up the gully on the east side and down the gully on the west side from the main summit towards Patchellhytta cabin. Here there is also a high risk of slip-sliding and the risk of bergschrund immediately below the exit from the gully.
Ascent:	Head from the cabin straight towards the cleft that lies between the north summit and the main summit. Then ski gently down to about 50 metres lower on the east side, before taking off your skis and following a steep gully up towards the summit area. The snow quality will decide whether you need crampons and/or an ice axe to make the ascent. The highest summit is the one to the west.
Descent:	The usual route back down is the same way as you went up. Even this offers challenging skiing. But one of the ultimate ski lines in the Sunnmøre Alps has a vertical drop of 800 metres from the summit and straight down the gullies to Patchellhytta cabin with an incline of 40 to 50 degrees! This line requires safe snow conditions as well as advanced skiing skills. If you are up to it, the line is really spectacular in fantastic surroundings.

Two alternative routes up and down from Store Smørskredtind.
Photo: Eirik Vaage

Skiing across the glacier at Brekketindbreen. Slogen in the background. Photo: Eirik Vaage

3.11 STORE BREKKETIND (1578 m)

FROM PATCHELLHYTTA

Store Brekketind is not among the most visited mountains, since the summit also presents climbing challenges. But the view towards Slogen and Jakta is spectacular, and the descent is fun.

Time: 3 hours.

Distance: 3 km.

Vertical ascent: 750 m.

Equipment: Helmet, shovel, probe, transceiver, alpine touring or telemark skis and winter clothing. To climb up the final 50 metres you will need crampons, an ice axe and some safety equipment.

Hazards: Risk of avalanches on the approach to the Brekketind glacier and in the gully up from the glacier towards the col. There is also a risk of crevasses, especially in the transition between the steep and gentler sections of the glacier and in the transition between the glacier itself and the mountain.

Ascent: Head north from the cabin towards Brekketindbotnen, before traversing steeply upwards the plateau on the Brekketindbreen. Follow this glacier towards a distinct cleft west of Store Brekketind. Go through the col and follow the snow flank and gullies a little way up. If you are planning to reach the summit, you will need climbing gear.

Descent: The most common route back down is the same way as you went up. But there is also a great alternative line down onto the Gullmor glacier from the col with inclines of up to 50 degrees. Skiing this line makes great demands on both snow quality and skiing skills. From the Gullmorbreen you must head south, up a short col, before you aim for Steinreset and glide back down to the cabin.

A crisp clear February day at Store Brekketind. Photo: Eirik Vaage

3.12   KVITEGGA (1717 m)

FROM THE RV655 IN NIBBEDALEN

If we exclude Tafjordfjella (in the eastern inner region of Sunnmøre), Kvitegga is the highest peak in the Sunnmøre Alps, and it offers great ski trips from various sides. Here we describe the most common route. Since the valley road through Norangsdalen is often closed due to avalanches for long periods during the winter (signs on the main road in Ørsta town centre provide updated information), this trip is usually made during the spring.

Time:	4 hours.
Distance:	6 km.
Vertical ascent:	1400 m.
Equipment:	Helmet, shovel, probe, transceiver, alpine touring or telemark skis and winter clothing.
Hazards:	Risk of avalanches, especially early in the winter.
Approach:	Follow the RV655 from Ørsta town centre to Sæbø. Take the ferry Sæbø-Lekneset and drive on up the Norangsdal. About 3.5 km after you have passed the newly-renovated Villa Norangdal hotel high up on the right-hand side of the road, you will find a car park. From this parking place in the Nibbedal valley there is wonderful skiing terrain up the Snødal valley. Traverse towards the right at a height of about 1000-1100 metres in the direction of Blåfjellet. Aim now for Høgd 1584, and then continue northwards along the ridge in easy terrain to the summit.
Descent:	The most common route back down is the same way as you went up. This is a moderate descent, with an incline that is mostly below 30 degrees. If you have access to transport in the Kjellstaddal valley (which lies to the north of the RV60 in Langedalen/Hornindalen), you can make a round trip. To do so, first ski south a short distance along the summit plateau, before dropping down into the Kjellstaddal. Now you can either put your skins back on and ascend the summit of the majestic peak Hornindalsrokken (1526m), or simply ski down the valley until you reach the main road. The descent from Hornindalsrokken is also via the Kjellstaddal.

The normal route up onto Kvitegga. Norangsdalen in the valley bottom.
Photo: Helge Standal

Having fun on skis heading down towards Snødalen.
Photo: Arnfinn Tønnesen

Speed and excitement in majestic surroundings. Photo: Ståle Johan Aklestad

3.13   EIDSKYRKJA (1482 m)

Time: 2-3 hours.
Distance: 4 km.
Vertical ascent: 1100 m.
Equipment: Helmet, shovel, probe, transceiver, alpine touring or telemark skis and winter clothing.
Hazards: Difficult to find one's bearings round the summit in poor visibility. Little risk of avalanches if you keep to the centre of the Blåbreen glacier, but be aware of the steep slopes to the west of the glacier.
Ascent: Head for the glacier and cruise up the gentle, inviting slope. The terrain levels out shortly before you go up onto the glacier itself, which has an incline of 25 degrees to begin with, but which gradually becomes flatter as you approach the summit plateau. From here there is a gentle rise of about 1 km south to the summit cairn.
Descent: The most common route back down is the same way as you went up. In good spring snow conditions you can cruise all the way back down to the summer farm. But you can also traverse to the left as you approach the flatter terrain below the glacier. When you stop, you can put your skins back on and follow the route described below, up to the summit of Lisje Eidskyrkja.

3.14   LISJE EIDSKYRKJA (1243 m)

Time: 2 hours.
Distance: 3 km.
Vertical ascent: 850 m.
Equipment: Helmet, shovel, probe, transceiver, alpine touring or telemark skis and winter clothing.
Hazards: Risk of avalanches east of the col. Cornice along the top ridge. Extreme risk of avalanches and of slip-sliding if you choose to descend down the north face.

ALPINE SKI TOURING STARTING FROM SKINNVIKSÆTRA IN AUSTEFJORD

The Austefjord area is not as well-known as the Hjørundfjord area among outdoor enthusiasts. True enough the mountains here are not as reminiscent of the Alps, but the Austefjord is one of the most underestimated areas of natural beauty in the region. It offers excellent opportunities for both fjord and river paddling, cragging and not least alpine ski touring in fantastic surroundings. Here we describe two of the most popular ski mountains in the area, both of which are approached from Skinnviksætra summer pasture: follow the E39 (from September 2012) from Volda to Fyrde at the end of the Austefjord. Take the RV655 for about 2 km round the other side of the fjord, before turning off left on a farm road/toll road. This is the first seter road to be cleared by snowploughs in the spring, and then you can make a steep drive all the way up to Skinnsviksætra at a height of 400m. In this way you can very quickly get to within striking distance of both Eidskyrkja and Lisje Eidskyrkja. If you are in reasonably good shape, you can make the summits of both of these in the space of a fine spring day.

Ascent: The first part of the route is the same as the route to Eidskyrkja, but you must traverse
           towards the southwest when you are level with the east ridge of Lisje Eidskyrkja. Follow
           the valley south of the ridge all the way until you come up onto a distinct col. From here
           you can follow the ridge to the summit.

Descent: The most usual route back down is the same way as you went up, but it is also common to
           choose steeper, more direct alternatives down towards the valley to the south, if condi-
           tions allow it. On days with absolutely no risk of avalanches, Lisje Eidskyrkja offers a re-
           ally challenging descent for the experienced skier. Drop off the top cornice and down the
           steep north face. Follow a band of snow towards the right, above steep crags and precipi-
           ces, until you enter the distinct narrow gully in the north face. Here the incline approac-
           hes 50 degrees. Ski down the gully and out onto flatter and more open terrain towards the
           seter.

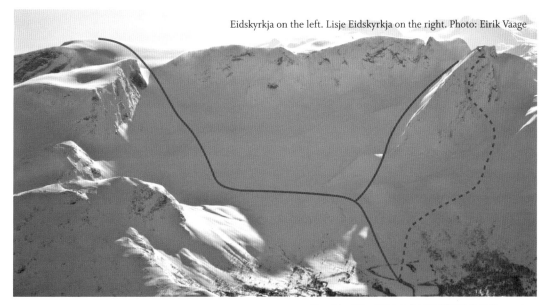

Eidskyrkja on the left. Lisje Eidskyrkja on the right. Photo: Eirik Vaage

On the way down Blåbreen glacier. Photo: Arnfinn Tønnesen

3.15 ROMEDALSTINDEN (1295 m)

This mountain is a particularly popular destination for an evening trip in May/June after the track to the seter at Steinstøylen has been opened for traffic. It is fine to start at about seven p.m. on a summer evening, so that you can enjoy the sunset out at sea while you are sitting on the summit.

Time:	2-3 hours.
Distance:	3 km.
Vertical ascent:	900 m from Steinstøylen.
Equipment:	Helmet, shovel, probe, transceiver, alpine touring or telemark skis and winter clothing.
Hazards:	Early in the summer the snow has usually become so hard-packed that there is little risk of avalanches. However, beware of crevasses having formed on the steepest and narrowest part of the snow glacier. Possible cornice on the top ridge. The top ridge is not difficult, but requires a good sense of balance.
Approach:	Take the RV655 from the town centre of Ørsta in the direction of Sæbø. After about 4 km, do not cross the bridge at Høgebrua, but drive straight on for about 7 km up the Follestaddal valley towards Kolåsen. Just before you reach Kolåsen itself, turn left onto the toll road up Romedalen. Follow the seter road up this beautiful valley for about 7 km until you can park at the pasture at Steinstøylen. Tie your skis to your sac and follow a fairly well defined path past the cabins, through a small wood and on up the lowest col between Hallehornet and Romedalstinden. Here you can usually put on your skis and traverse east for several hundred metres before climbing steeply up the glacier itself heading south. Follow the glacier south in undulating terrain, which gradually becomes steeper up towards the col east of the peak of Romedalstinden. Leave your skis in the col and climb to the left of the ridge until you reach some gully formations. Follow these up to a foresummit. Then scramble a couple of hundred metres along the ridge until you arrive at the summit cairn. Now sit down and soak in the last rays of the sun as it sets way out to sea over Breisundet in the west.
Descent:	The normal route back down is the same way as you went up. The incline is no more than 35 degrees, but beware of possible crevasses in the narrowest section of the glacier.

All these trips can naturally be made on foot during the summer, but then usually along slightly different routes. Be aware of crevasses that might appear on some of these mountains as the snow melts during the summer.

Sliding along the top ridge of Romedalstinden. Photo: Arnfinn Tønnesen

Soaking up the last rays as the sun sets over Breisundet. Brillevatnet in the foreground. Photo: Arnfinn Tønnesen

4 SKI AREAS

If the risk of avalanches is too great in the high mountains or if you simply want to have a day skiing the pistes, it may be a good idea to take a trip to one of the many ski centres in the Sunnmøre Alps.
www.alpepasset.no is a joint project involving all the ski facilities in Sunnmøre whereby you purchase a pass that allows access to all the centres in the project. All the prices below apply for adults in the 2010/2011 season. Note that most of the ski centres also hire out skiing equipment.

The Alpepasset pass provides access to:
8 ski centres
36 lifts
70 trails
Plenty of backcountry skiing
You can also choose from 2 to 10 days of your own choice at a variety of prices. 5 days of your own choice cost NOK 1425.
Price for the whole season: NOK 4150.

A powder run on Strandafjellet. Photo: Mattias Fredriksson

4.1 ØRSTA SKISENTER (Bondalseidet)

Approach: Drive about 15 km from Ørsta town centre along the RV655 towards Sæbø. Turn left at sign indicating ski centre.

Season: December – April.

Open: Tuesday-Friday: 18-21. Saturday & Sunday: 10-16.

Lifts: A children's pull by the lower lift. A tow and a chair lift to Eitrefjellet. It takes about 10 minutes to skate to the next T-hook at Nottane towards Veirahaldet.

Food/drink: A base cafeteria and one on the summit of Eitrefjellet. Toilets and simple refreshments.

Priorities: Family, with prepared runs for alpine, telemark and snowboard.

Vertical drop: 350m in the main facility. 150m in the rear section of the facility.

Park: The facility has a few rails and jumps.

Nordic: In daylight 12 km of trails to Åmskaret. In evenings 5 km of floodlit trails.

Prices: All-day pass: NOK 300. Evening pass: NOK 190. Season ticket: NOK 3200. Alpepass.

Telephone: +47 70 04 01 60

Web: www.orstaskisenter.no

Comments: In 2006 Ørsta skisenter was chosen as one of the ten best ski centres by the skiing magazine Fri Flyt, in spite of the fact that operations are run entirely by volunteers. The ski centre is known for its good opportunities for backcountry and glade skiing and alpine ski touring direct from the ski lifts. Later in the winter the rear section of the facility is opened, providing access to relatively easy summits with both slopes and crags of various sizes. Snowfalls vary considerably from year to year, but the facility also has good capacity for snow production. The prepared trails normally offer good conditions.

ALPINE SKI TOURING FROM THE SKI LIFT

VEIRAHALDET (1206 moh.)

Approach: Take the ski lift to the top station on Nottane. From there you can follow the ridge all the way to the summit. Beware of cornices on your right as you ascend and the large cornice on the left at the summit.

Vertical metres: From the top station it is only 500 vertical metres to the summit, but you have a vertical drop of 850 metres from the summit to the base station. On the way down, experienced skiers can make a detour via the cliffs above Trollkoppen – if conditions allow it. An alternative route down via Frølandsdalen to Follestaddalen offers a vertical drop of about 1000 metres, but from there you will need a car to get back to the ski area.

BLÅTINDEN (1182 moh.)

Approach: Take the ski lift to the top station on Nottane. From there you go diagonally south, towards the right and Trollkoppen. From there you ascend steeply to the summit in terrain that is subject to avalanches.

Vertical metres: Roughly the same as from Veirhaldet. The mountain offers magnificent descents towards Trollkoppen in terrain that is subject to avalanches. You can also head in the direction of Stokke in the Bondal valley, from where you will require a car to return to the ski area.

Skiers on the top ridge of Blåtinden. Photo: Stian Wiik

4.2   VOLDA SKISENTER (Reset)

Approach: Follow the RV651 up out of Volda town centre. At the roundabout take the second exit
               into Vikebygdvegen. Continue until you have climbed uphill into the mountains. A few
               hundred metres after the road has levelled out, you will see the sign for Volda skisenter on
               your left.
Season: December – March/April.
Open: Tuesday-Friday: 18-21. Saturday & Sunday: 1030-1630.
Lifts: A Poma and two children's tows.
Food/drink: A base cafe with simple refreshments.
Priorities: Family.
Vertical drop: 300m.
Park: Some rails and small jumps.
Nordic: 3.5 km of floodlit trails.
Prices: All-day pass: NOK 290. Evening pass: NOK 180. Season ticket: NOK 2700. Alpepass.
Telephone: +47 70 07 84 00
Web: www.voldaskisenter.no

Comments: Volda skisenter is the smallest of the centres in the area, and is operated by volunteers.
               Reset prioritises families and has built up good facilities for this group, including a new
               family tow installed in 2010. The facility offers good opportunities for glade skiing. The
               centre does not produce artificial snow, and there is a risk of it having to close temporarily
               during winters with little snow.

ALPINE SKI TOURING FROM THE SKI LIFT

From the top of the ski lift you see Grøthornet to the north, which you can reach after just a short ski
trip. It is also an easy trip from Grøthornet to Melshornet (803m), with excellent views of Ørsta and
the surrounding mountains. From the summits of these gentle mountains there are several descents to
choose from: back to the ski tow, down to the road over Krøvelseidet or down to the centres of either
Volda or Ørsta via the Dinglavatnet lake (reservoir).

Melshornet in the
centre of the picture.
Saudehornet in the
background.
Photo: Helge Standal

4.3 SUNNMØRSALPANE SKIARENA
(Fjellsætra in Sykkylven)

Approach: From Ørsta you can drive north on the E39 to Festøya. Take the ferry to Hundeidvik, and follow the signs to Stranda until you reach Sykkylven. Head south on the RV60 from the centre of Sykkylven towards Stranda for about 30km. Turn left off the main road at a bridge, where the Skiarena is clearly signposted. From Ålesund you can drive north on the E39 and take the Magerholm-Sykkylven ferry before heading on to Sunnmørsalpane Skiarena.

Season: December – April.
Open: Monday, Wednesday & Thursday: 18-21. Saturday & Sunday: 10-16.
Lifts: 5 lifts of different types.
Food/drink: Hot and cold food available at Fjellseterstova at the base cafe.
Priorities: A variety of facilities for all the family. Excellent floodlighting.
Vertical drop: 400m.
Park: Well developed park with rails and jumps.
Nordic: 25 km of prepared trails.
Prices: All-day pass: NOK 300. Evening pass: NOK 200. Season ticket: NOK 2950. Alpepass.
Telephone: +47 70 25 06 06
Web: www.sunnmorsalpane.no

Comments: Fjellsætra is certainly less famous than the neighbouring ski area Strandafjellet, but it offers a great skiing experience for everyone regardless of age and skills. The groomed runs are even accessible at nights on weekdays, due to excellent floodlighting. But the main attraction is the backcountry terrain that you will find directly from the lift in all directions. To the left of the intermediate station you can soon find pretty demanding glade skiing. If you take the lift to the top station, you will find steep backcountry terrain with jumpable cliffs on both sides. If you want to make an extra effort, a 2-300 metre vertical climb will take you from the top station to the summits of Langfjella (1118m) or Revsdalshornet (1006m). The facility has good capacity for snowmaking.

4.4   STRANDAFJELLET SKISENTER

Approach: From Ørsta you can drive north on the E39 to Festøya. Take the ferry to Hundeidvik, and follow the signs to Stranda. Do not cross the large bridge at Ikkornes/Sykkylven, but keep straight ahead at the roundabout, which will save you an expensive toll charge. On your way to the centre of Stranda, you cannot miss Stranda Skisenter. From Ålesund you can drive north on the E39 and take the Magerholm-Sykkylven ferry before heading on to Stranda Skisenter.

Season: December – April.

Open: Daily 10-16 and Monday-Thursday 18-21.

Lifts: 7 lifts of different types.

Food/drink: Base cafe. Licensed pavilions serving food at the top stations on both sides.

Priorities: Off-piste. Also a summer programme with refreshments and activities.

Vertical drop: 800m.

Park: Fairly well developed park with rails and jumps.

Nordic: 3 km of floodlit trails and 5 km of prepared tracks.

Prices: All-day pass: NOK 330. Evening pass: NOK 205. Season ticket: NOK 3300. Alpepass.

Telephone: +47 70 26 02 12

Web: www.strandafjellet.no

Comments: Stranda Skisenter is the largest ski area in the Sunnmøre Alps, particularly well known for its backcountry terrain. Strandafjellet offers everyone the chance to try powder snow, regardless of skills and experience. Often there are only one or two prepared runs for those who prefer that, while the rest of the runs are left unprepared after the last snowfall. On the Roald side a new express lift was opened in 2011 with a large pavilion just below the summit of Roaldshornet (1230m). From here there are challenging backcountry runs in all directions. On the Furset side you can run off-piste straight from the lift. Several of the areas demand good skiing skills, and you must be able to assess the risk of avalanches. The facility has good capacity for snowmaking.

Big air overlooking the fjord. Photo: Eirik Vaage

A powder run in the woods. Photo: Einar Engdal

4.5 STORDAL ALPINSENTER (Arena Overøye)

Approach: Follow the E39 from Ørsta or the E136 from Ålesund to Moa and turn off here onto the E39 to Trondheim. When you get to Sjøholt, turn off right onto the RV650 towards Geiranger/Stordal. From the centre of Stordal drive for 5.6 km before you turn left. Follow the road for about 9 km to the ski centre.

Season: December – April.

Open: Tuesday and Friday 19-21. Saturday and Sunday 10.30-16.30

Lifts: Two children's tows, a Poma and a T-bar.

Food/drink: Simple refreshments in base cafe.

Priorities: Family and backcountry.

Vertical drop: 400m.

Park: Some rails and jumps.

Nordic: 4-5 km of prepared trails.

Prices: All-day pass: NOK 300. Evening pass: NOK 200. Season ticket: NOK 2900. Alpepass.

Telephone: +47 70 27 83 90

Web: www.stordalalpinsenter.no

On the way down from Overøystølen. Photo: Einar Engdal

4.6 ØRSKOGFJELLET SKISENTER

Approach: Follow the E39 from Ørsta or the E136 from Ålesund to Moa and turn off here onto the E39 to Trondheim. Follow the E39 through Sjøholt and up into the mountains. The facility will appear on your right immediately after you pass the highest point on the road. From the top lift station at 700m you can ski to the summit of Sandtinden (1065m) and enjoy a great backcountry run back down.

Season: December – April.

Open: Tuesday and Thursday 18-21. Saturday and Sunday 10.30-16.30

Lifts: A Poma , a T-bar and a magic carpet.

Food/drink: Simple refreshments in base cafe.

Priorities: Family and backcountry.

Vertical drop: 400m.

Park: Some rails and jumps.

Nordic: 2.5 km of prepared trails.

Prices: All-day pass: NOK 280. Evening pass: NOK 170. Season ticket: NOK 2800. Alpepass.

Telephone: +47 95 09 63 33

Web: www.orskogfjellet.no

Ørskogfjell

4.7 HARPEFOSSEN SKISENTER

Approach: From Volda you take the ferry to Folkestad and continue on the E39 (new classification after Sept 2012) over Stigedalen until you reach the roundabout in Eid. Take the second exit and follow the RV15 for about 5 km. Turn right onto the RV661 and drive for 3 km, before continuing on the RV61 for 2 km. Turn right again and drive the last 500 metres to the ski area.

Season: December – April.

Open: Tuesday, Thursday & Friday 17.30-20.30. Saturday and Sunday 10.30-16.30

Lifts: Two Pomas , a family tow and two pony lifts.

Food/drink: Simple refreshments in base cafe.

Priorities: Family and backcountry.

Vertical drop: 500m.

Park: Some rails and jumps.

Nordic: 15 km of prepared trails.

Prices: All-day pass: NOK 300. Evening pass: NOK 230. Season ticket: NOK 3200. Alpepass.

Telephone: +47 57 86 25 50

Web: www.harpefossen.no

Harpefossen Skisenter kan tilby
• 6 heisar • 13 nedfartar • Terrengpark • Skileikområde• Store områder for laussnøkøyring
• 2 km lysløype • 10 km rundløype langrenn • Turløyper frå toppen av fjellheisen • Skiskyttarstadion
• To serveringsstadar• Skiutleige og butikk• Flomlys og snøproduksjon i hovudtrasear og terrengpark

4.8   STRYN SKISENTER

Approach: From Oslo follow the E6 towards Trondheim and turn left at Otta onto the RV15 road to Lom and Stryn. Drive through the centre of Stryn, take the first exit at the roundabout and turn right immediately after the petrol station. From Volda you take the E39 (after Sept 2012) in the direction of Stryn / Oslo. About 6.5 km after the centre of Hornindal turn left onto the RV15. Continue on this road until you are approaching the centre of Stryn. Turn left just before the petrol station onto a farm road. Follow this road up through a housing estate until you reach the ski centre.

Season: December – April.

Open: Wednesday-Friday 17-21. Saturday and Sunday 11-16.

Lifts: Two T-bars and two children's tows.

Food/drink: Simple refreshments in base cafe.

Priorities: Park facilities.

Vertical drop: 650m.

Park: Well-equipped park area. Big air bag, large and small jumps and rails.

Nordic: 20 - 30 km of prepared trails. 2 km floodlit trails from the base station.

Prices: All-day pass: NOK 310. Evening pass: NOK 200. Season ticket: NOK 3200. Alpepass.

Telephone: +47 57 87 11 15

Web: www.strynskisenter.no

A crisp clear winter's day on the ski tow. Photo: Jo Bergersen

4.9 STRYN SOMMARSKISENTER

Approach: From Oslo follow the E6 towards Trondheim and turn left at Otta onto the RV15 towards Lom and Stryn. Drive to Grotli on the Strynefjell mountain pass. You can either turn left onto the old mountain pass RV259 (gamle Strynefjellsvegen) when this is open for traffic or drive over the mountain pass and through the three tunnels. Immediately after leaving the last tunnel, just before the main road starts to descend into the valley, turn left onto the old mountain pass RV259 (gamle Strynefjellsvegen) signposted to Grotli. From Volda you take the E39 (after Sept 2012) in the direction of Stryn / Oslo. About 6.5 km after the centre of Hornindal turn left onto the RV15. Continue on this road through the centre of Stryn. After climbing the hairpins, turn right onto the old mountain pass marked RV259 (gamle Strynefjellsvegen) signposted to Grotli, immediately before the first tunnel. Continue until you reach the ski centre. If you need overnight accommodation, we recommend the legendary Folven campsite at the foot of the mountains on the Stryn side.

Season: End of May – mid-August.
Open: Daily 10-16.
Lifts: A chair lift and a T-bar.
Food/drink: Cafe with meals served outdoors on first floor of the service centre. Also a great place to sunbathe.
Priorities: Summer skiing.
Vertical drop: 600m. Base station: 1080m. Top station: 1600m.
Park: If sufficient snow.
Nordic: 10 km of prepared trails at top of the Tystigbreen glacier.
Prices: All-day pass: NOK 320. Season ticket: NOK 2990. Alpepass N/A.
Telephone: +47 91 53 10 61
Web: www.strynskisenter.no

Perfect conditions at the Stryn summer ski area. Photo: Henning Heimlid

5 ICE CLIMBING

Most of the Sunnmøre Alps lie close to the coast, giving mild, wet winters. Therefore there are normally not stable conditions for ice climbing in the area. But during the harshest winter months (December – February) there may be brief periods of cold weather that provide good ice. It is usually a case of being in the right place at the right time.

GRADING

WI1:   Fairly flat ice slopes, where you only need crampons and an ice axe to complete the climb.
WI2:   60-70 degree massive ice in short pitches. Good rests, stances and protection.
WI3:   60-70 degree massive ice. Good rests, stances and protection.
WI4:   75-80 degree massive ice. Satisfactory rests, stances and adequate protection.
WI5:   85-90 degree massive ice. Possibly variable ice quality, occasionally very steep and sustained, but rests and adequate stances. Nevertheless can be difficult to protect.
WI6:   Extremely steep and sustained, without rests. Hanging stances. Ice quality can vary   and opportunities for protection may be dubious.
WI7:   Steep, thin ice of poor quality and poor anchors. Poor protection.

5.1 BREITEIGFOSSEN

Grading: WI5+
Length: 3 pitches. 1st pitch involves medium climbing with some mushroom formations. Good stances. 2nd pitch presents sustained climbing at WI3-4 with many small mushrooms. 3rd pitch represents sustained climbing at WI5 up partly free-hanging icicle. The route flattens out after the top pillar.
Equipment: Helmet, harness, two ropes (60m), crampons, two ice axes, ice screws and winter clothing.
Hazards: Exposed to ice-falls and avalanches from the top. Avoid the river bed on the approach, as this is subject to avalanches.
First ascent: Åsmund Vaage and Tommi Räty, February 2010.
Approach: Take the Volda-Lauvstad ferry and follow the RV652 towards Syvde. After about 30 km you reach Rovde, and a range of massive walls appear on your left-hand side. Park the car at the farm immediately below Breiteigfossen. The shortest approach is to follow the river bed all the way from the car to the entry point, but if there is a risk of avalanches, it is safer to follow the ridge to the right of the river. The easiest return to the entry point is via an ice and snow gully 60 metres to the left of the waterfall. From there you can follow the river or the ridge back to the car.

Climbing a typical mushroom on the 2nd pitch of Breiteigfossen. Photo. Tommy Räty

5.2 TYSSEFOSSEN

This is actually two waterfalls: Nedstefossen and Øvstefossen.

Grading: WI3
Length:
Nedstefossen: One pitch with simple, gentle climbing, grade II.
Øvstefossen: 2 pitches. 1st pitch has a section of more demanding climbing if the most challenging route is chosen, but there are also easier alternatives. Good stances. You can also choose steepness on the 2nd pitch, but this is somewhat easier in any case, especially if you traverse towards the right.
Equipment: Helmet, harness, two ropes (60m), crampons, two ice axes, ice screws and winter clothing.
Hazards: Thin ice here and there.
Approach: Follow the E39 (after September 2012) from the centre of Volda through the Rotsethorn and the Hjartå tunnels along the eastern side of the Austefjord, and on towards Stryn. Turn off left just before the Kvivs tunnel and follow the RV41 in the direction of Bjørke. Swing up to the right just before you get to Bjørke. 5 min walk to Nedstefossen, 15 min to Øvstefossen. After the final pitch on Øvstefossen you can go through the woods on the right and climb or rappel back down onto the plateau between the two waterfalls. Then a short walk back to the car.

5.3 FOLKESTADFERJA

Grading: WI4
Length: 3 pitches. 1st pitch is steepest. Good stances. 2nd pitch is less steep. 3rd pitch rounds out towards the exit point.
Equipment: Helmet, harness, two ropes (60m), crampons, two ice axes, ice screws and winter clothing.
Hazards: Thin ice here and there. Possible risk of avalanches.
First ascent: Stig Helset, Leif Strand and Åsmund Vaage, January 2004.
Approach: From Volda to Folkestad, take the ferry, whose wake gave the first ascenders the idea for the name. Drive your car or ski up along the east side of the Folkestadvatnet lake (315m), to just beyond the end of the lake. Gradually two ice lines will appear in the wall up towards Sætrehornet (760m). "Folkestadferja" is the second, steepest and longest ice line on the mountain. Allow almost an hour for the approach up to the entry point (450m), which is a steep snow slope below a 50-metre wide ice wall. After the exit point it is easiest to return on foot via Sætrehornet, northwards and then down the hillside back to the lake.

Classic climbing on the 2nd pitch of Folkestadferja. Photo: Stig J. Helset

5.4   DEI SJU SYSTRENE

Grading: WI6
Length: 400 metres. The first 100 metres are easy climbing, but the final 300 metres present
                sustained steep climbing.
Equipment: Helmet, harness, two ropes (60m), crampons, two ice axes, ice screws and winter
                clothing.
Hazards: Thin ice here and there. Possible risk of avalanches, and not enough time.
First ascent: Bjarte Bø, Henki Flatlandsmo, Eiliv Ruud and Sindre Sæter 1.2.2011.
Approach in winter: Follow the E39 from Ørsta or the E136 from Ålesund to Moa and then turn off on
                the E39 towards Trondheim. Turn right when you get to Sjøholt and follow the RV650 via
                Stordal to Liabygda and take the ferry from Linge to Eidsdal. Then follow the RV63 across
                the mountain pass and down the hairpins of Ørnesvingane to Geiranger. From the centre
                of Geiranger you will need a boat out to where Dei sju systrene cascades into the fjord.
                Contact Destinasjon Geiranger for boat transport. The waterfall is on the right-hand side
                of the fjord and is the left-hand section of Dei sju systrene. Return down the waterfall on
                Abalakov (V-thread) anchors or go down to Knivsflå mountain farm to the right of the
                waterfall and follow the path down to the fjord.

5.5   SJUSOVARSYSTRENE

Grading: WI6
Length: 400 metres. The first 100 metres are easy climbing, but the final 300 metres present a
                great deal of steep and technically difficult climbing.
Equipment: Helmet, harness, two ropes (60m), crampons, two ice axes, ice screws and winter
                clothing.
Hazards: Thin ice here and there. Possible risk of avalanches, and not enough time.
First ascent: Sigurd Felde, Anders Mordal and Eivind Nordeide 2.2.2011.
Approach in winter: See the instructions for Dei sju systrene. Sjusovarsystrene lies on the right-hand side
                of the fjord and is the right-hand section of Dei sju systrene. Return down the waterfall
                on Abalakov (V-thread) anchors or go down to Knivsflå mountain farm to the right of the
                waterfall and follow the path down to the fjord.

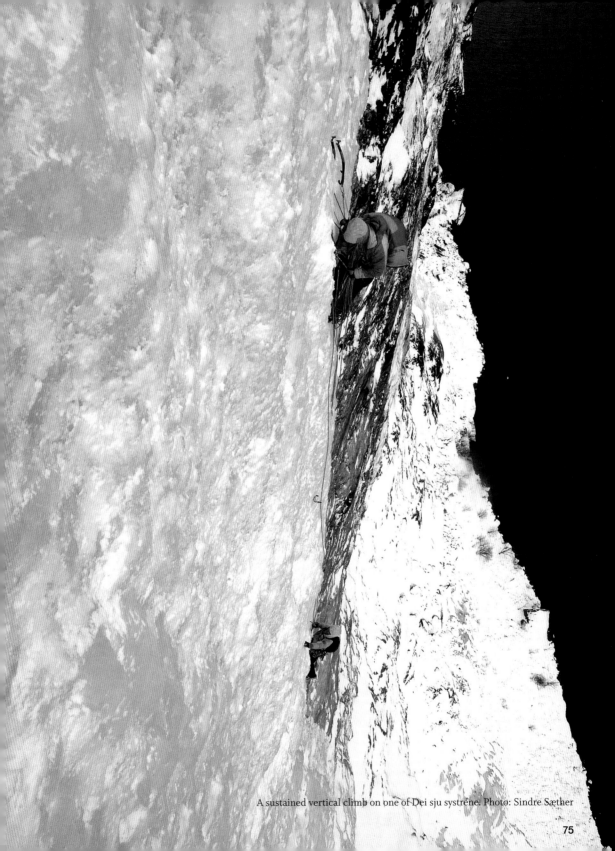

A sustained vertical climb on one of Dei sju systrene. Photo: Sindre Sæther

Climbing the final section of Alterbekken.
Photo: Audun Rønebæk Stikbakke

5.6   ALTERBEKKEN

Grading: WI6
Length: 350 metres.
Equipment: Helmet, harness, two ropes (60m), crampons, two ice axes, ice screws, stoppers and win-
                ter clothing.
Hazards: Ice-falls, difficult to assess the ice quality and not enough time.
First ascent: Bjarte Bø and Sindre Sæter, February 2011.
Approach in winter: See the instructions for Dei sju systrene. Alterbekken lies further down the fjord
                on the left-hand side. The route goes to the far left between several ice lines that come
                down at Skagen. Jump ashore on the rocks at the start of the route. Here you can protect
                with stoppers before the climbing on the ice begins. 1st pitch presents 60 metres of easy
                climbing to the stance in the hole to the right in the waterfall. 2nd – 4th pitches present
                steep climbing up pillars, before reaching an easier section in the middle. The final ascent
                goes up a steep section to the right, which turns into a narrower pillar towards the end.
                You finish on a rock ledge, where you can belay in trees. Return down the waterfall on
                Abalakov (V-thread) anchors or go along the summer path from the Skageflå mountain
                farm to Homlong and then follow the road back to the centre of Geiranger.

A carpet of mist below Slogen. Jakta in the background.
Photo: Per Børge Flemsæter

6 MOUNTAIN HIKING

In the old days the mountains were considered to be useless and even dangerous. The local farmers therefore kept their movements in the mountains to a minimum. Only when they were forced to do so in connection with herding their sheep and goats before the winter did they venture high into the mountains, but rarely up onto the summits. Nevertheless the British climbing pioneers who visited Sunnmøre towards the end of the 1800s found cairns on several spectacular high peaks in the region. This shows that at least some local enthusiasts had discovered the excitement and joy of climbing right to the top even earlier than that. But these were the exceptions that confirmed the rule that the locals in general kept their distance from the mountains until well into the twentieth century. In the decade after the last world war it became more common to go mountain hiking simply for the sake of recreation. In the last couple of decades interest has really exploded. On any given day with fine weather a hundred or so people can visit the most well-known summits in the area. The hiking season in Sunnmøre usually lasts from April/May to October/November. All the estimates below regarding time apply to the ascent, and naturally they are approximate. If safety equipment is required, this is specified in the description of the trip in question. In any case, our advice is that you wear a pair of good hiking boots and have warm clothing with you in your backpack.

A lofty vantage point above the beach at Hoddevika on Stad. Photo: Eirik Vaage

6.1   JØNSHORNET (1419 m)

Time: 4 hours
Distance: 3 km
Vertical ascent: 1200 metres

Approach: Take the E39 north from Ørsta or south from Ålesund via the Solavågen-Festøya ferry, and turn off in Barstadvika towards Erdalen, which is clearly signposted. Follow the road and later the toll road to Melbøsætra summer pasture. From the car park there is a distinct path towards Molladalen. At the gateway to the valley itself, the so-called Molladalsporten, the path becomes very steep and you will find a chain to hold on to. The view of the whole range of peaks is now at its very best! Follow the path until you reach the Storevatnet lake, where you turn sharply up the grassy slopes west of the Jønshornsrenna gully. Follow the steep gully all the way up to the col on the west ridge, and beware of falling rocks and the risk of slipping – especially if there is still snow about. Now climb the ridge towards the right up to the summit or cross the glacier. The view from the top is among the most spectacular in the Sunnmøre Alps.

Descent: A fine alternative is to return via the summit of Rametinden. Climb the west ridge from the summit down into Ramoskaret, before heading up onto Rametinden. Here you follow the ridge to Breidaksla, then along the path to Gamlestøylen summer pasture. From there you follow the path along the stream down to the road at Vollane, which is about 2 km from the E39 in Barstadvika. The disadvantage of this alternative is that you must now walk 3 km along the road to fetch the car at Melbøsætra – if you have not made other arrangements.

6.2   MOHNS TOPP (1340 m)

Time: 4 hours
Distance: 4 km
Vertical ascent: 1130 metres

Approach: Follow the same route as described for Jønshornet as far as the Storevatn lake in Molladalen. Go along the north side of the lake on a good path. As you approach the eastern end of the lake, you should go up to the left in the direction of Mohnsrenna. On the way to the gully you will pass the enormous boulder called Børresteinen. The path to Mohnsrenna is mainly pretty obvious, but it is very steep, and you must beware of rock falls and slipping on the remains of the snow which often lies until well into the summer. Safely up on the col, you head to the right and climb the ridge south to the summit. Many people like to protect themselves by using a rope on this final section. From the top there is a magnificent view in every direction. Among others you will see the pinnacle Bladet down to your left. You will need climbing gear to reach the top of this pinnacle.

Descent: If someone can pick you up at Ytre-Standal, we recommend that as the final destination for this trip. In that case, go back down the same way to the eastern end of the lake. Then keep to the east of it, and head up the Grøneskaret col south of Grønetinden. From the col you can follow a marked path down to the little seter in Ytre-Standaldalen and on back down to the hamlet and the road.

On the way up towards Jønshornrenna. Photo: Ma Ortiz

On the way up towards Mohns topp. Bladet, Giganten and the Hjørundfjord in the background. Photo: Ma Ortiz

Molladalen. Jønshornet to the left, Randers topp in the centre and Mohns topp to the right. Photo: Helge Standal

On the way up the final section of east ridge on Liadalsnipa. Photo: Arnt Flatmo.

6.3   LIADALSNIPA (924 m)

Time: 2-3 hours
Distance: 2-3 km
Vertical ascent: 780 metres
Approach: Drive on the E39 from Ørsta towards Ålesund. About 7 km from the centre of Ørsta, turn
              off right at the sign «Halse 1.2 km»*. Park at the top farm in such a way that you do not
              obstruct the work of the farmer. Then follow the farm track which becomes a well defined
              path on the way up to the summit, which you can see all the way. When you reach the
              Nakkevatnet lake, you have two alternatives: the normal route up the west ridge or a
              more exciting trip up the east ridge. We describe the ascent up the east ridge and the
              descent down the west ridge. Follow the path along the north side of the lake, which will
              lead you up to the Nykkjavatnet lake. Now head west in easy terrain across Nipesletta. At
              the top of the grassy slope you face a steep col. Here you either rappel down with a rope
              or climb a detour down the gully on the south side, before you advance to the lowest point
              on the col. From here it is easy, but airy climbing over the ridge to the summit of Lia-
              dalsnipa itself. Some may choose to use a rope as protection here.
Descent: Follow the steep and exposed path down the north side, before you swing to the left
              and climb over onto the west ridge itself. You follow this down to Storhaugen, before
              returning to the Nakkevatnet lake. Equipped with a rope, most experienced hikers will
              manage this trip safely. However, we must emphasise that there is a considerable risk of
              falling, so do take care.

The normal route to Liadalsnipa to the right, the route to the east ridge to the left. Photo: Helge Standal

6.4 KJERRINGA (1130 m)

Time: 2-3 hours
Distance: 4-5 km
Vertical ascent: 800 metres
Approach: Turn off the RV655 up Mosmarkvegen before the bridge at Rossåbrua in the centre of Ørsta. Turn left onto the farm track/toll road in the lower part of the housing estate, and follow this for 7 km as far as Mossætra. The seter makes a good starting point for a number of mountain hikes, e.g. to Vassdalstinden and Åvasstinden. If you are heading for Kjerringa, you now take the path up to Fyldalheida. Then you can choose whether you take a steep route with no path over Rotbergshornet or follow a good path round this peak (see photo topos). Regardless of your choice you end up on the col towards Langedalen. Now follow a steep path up along the ridge towards Årsæterhornet, but traverse to the left in the direction of Kjerringa just before the ridge, and follow a gully up onto the ridge. Now follow the top ridge northwards, keeping slightly to the east side, until you are standing just below the summit. Then climb steeply up to the cairn.
Descent: If you have access to transport in Romedalen, you can make this an enjoyable round trip by heading down into this beautiful valley. You can see the whole return route from the summit.

Roteberghornet in the foreground. Kjerringa in the background. Photo: Stig J. Helset

On the way up towards Fyldalheida. Langedalen and Kjerringa in the background. Photo: Stig J. Helset

6.5 DALEGUBBEN (1344 m) / HOLMSHORNET (1198 m)

Time:	3 hours
Distance:	3 km
Vertical ascent:	1300 metres

Approach: Take the RV655 from the centre of Ørsta towards Sæbø. Turn left at the Rise farms just before the centre of Sæbø. Park beside a zig-zag gravel road that you can see on the hillside below the mountain from the main road. Follow the road a little way up before joining a distinct path up to Storenakken. The path leads you to the right towards Skonda-len, a valley which you are to follow all the way up to the col on the horizon. From there it is an easy climb up to the summit on the left. The view from Dalegubben offers fantastic opportunities for photography.

Descent: Go back to the col east of the summit. If you have plenty of time, a head for heights and perhaps some safety equipment, you can now head for the exotic Holmshornet peak. Follow the ridge eastwards, before making a lofty climb down to the col below the summit. Then balance on the narrow top ridge all the way to the cairn, and you will be able to look right down into the Hjørundfjord. Return the same way to the col below Dalegubben and follow Skondalen back down.

Dalegubben far left in background. Holmshornet out to the right. Photo: Stig J. Helset

View from Dalegubben. Holmshornet behind and to the left. Photo: Arild Berge

On the foresummit of Holmshornet, which is behind and to the left. Photo: Fred I. Somby

On the summit of Råna. Nordaustegga below to the right. Photo: Håvard Myklebust

6.6 RÅNA (1586 m) / URKEDALSTINDANE (1524 m)

Time: 4 hours
Distance: 6 km
Vertical ascent: 1360 metres
Approach: Take the RV655 from the centre of Ørsta towards Sæbø. Cross the fjord on the Sæbø-
                Lekneset ferry and continue along the RV655 for about 3 km as far as Urke. Follow the
                signpost to Urkedalen via a toll road and park just before Haukåssætra summer pasture.
                There is a well marked path into the Urkedal valley. After a while you enter the barren
                Nordkopen and here you cross a snowfield and go steeply up onto the col west of Midtre
                Regndalstind. Safely up on the col, you will see the long, gently ascending top ridge on
                the Råna- plateau. Follow this ridge all the way to the cairn.
Descent: On the way back, you can make a detour to Midtre Regndalstind, which is easy to reach
                from the south end of the Råna-plateau. If you have plenty of time, enjoy climbing on airy
                ridges and have safety equipment with you, you can continue southwards along the sharp
                ridge to Urkedalstindane. From the summit of Urkedalstindane you can now go down
                into Grøtdalen and on back to Haukåssætra. We emphasise that this particular descent is
                only suitable for experienced climbers.

The normal route up to Råna from Urkedalen via Nordkopen. Photo: Helge Standal

6.7 TRANDALHATTEN (1140 m)

Time: 2-3 hours
Distance: 2-3 km
Vertical ascent: 900 metres

Approach: Take the RV655 from the centre of Ørsta and take the ferry from Sæbø to Trandal. Drive up the farm road until you reach a sharp right-hand bend at about 250 m. Now turn left and go through the woods in the direction of the ridge that leads you up below the summit. The path becomes more distinct as you gain height. At 1000 metres you must go round to the left on the west side of the summit. Now go up onto the north col and climb to the top.

Descent: An enjoyable return trip is via Nesdalen, the valley which you can see to the west of you from the summit. If you are feeling fit enough, you can also climb the summit of Seljeneshornet and/or Nesstaven from Nesdalen. Safely back down at Nes, you follow a fine road along the shoreline the 2 km back to Trandal. If you need accommodation for the night or just some light refreshments, you can make a stop at the exotic hostelry Christian Gaard at Indre Trandal.

The normal route up to Trandalhatten from Trandaldalen. Photo: Helge Standal

View up the Hjørundfjord from the ascent up to Trandalhatten. Photo: Arnfinn Tønnesen

Molladalen. Photo: Arnfinn Tønnesen

7   ROCK CLIMBING

When it comes to climbing in the summer, there is one area that really stands out among all the others in the Sunnmøre Alps: Molladalen. This magnificent valley offers about 70 established climbing routes on relatively solid rock. The range of difficulty varies from 3 to 7, while the number of pitches varies from 2 to 6. You can approach the base camp beside the lake known as Storevatnet from three different valleys: Lisje-Standalssætra in Ytre-Standaldalen, Steinstøylen in Romedalen and Melbøsætra in Barstaddalen. We describe the latter. Drive north along the E39 from Ørsta or south from Ålesund via the ferry Solavågen-Festøya, and turn off the main road in Barstadvika towards Erdalen, which is clearly signposted. Follow the road and later a toll road up to Melbøsætra summer pasture. Take the well defined path towards Molladalen. As you enter Molladalsporten, you will see a row of peaks the sight of which you will never forget. Beside the lake there is ample room to set up your tent. If you do not have one, you can follow the path up onto the first ridge above the lake and settle down for the night in the cave below the big boulder Reiulf Steen. The hike up from the car park takes about an hour and a half. In what follows we describe a small, but varied selection of the many climbing routes in the valley. We begin with a couple of easy routes on Holtanna and Mohns topp, move on to some classics on the south wall of Jønshornet, before finishing off with a pair of challenging routes on the fantastic Krut-tårnet.

7.1 HOLTANNA VESTVEGGEN

Approach: Follow the path up from the base camp by the lake, past the overnight hollow under Reiulf Steen on a distinct ridge, then traverse a steep flank along the path towards the enormous Børresteinen. Now hike towards the col south of Holtanna, but veer to the left up steep slopes to the entry point on a sloping stony ledge. You can also climb Holtanna from the south (grading 5 -) – cf the photo topo.

Length: 120 metres

Grading: 6 -

First ascent: Jarle S. Bjørdal, Jon Hagen and Odd Staurset 1988.

Equipment: Helmet, climbing harness, climbing shoes, rope and a normal rack.

Description: 1st pitch goes up a distinct and fast firm solid dihedral. Stance on a good, vegetated ledge. 2nd pitch goes up a steep rib that gives excellent climbing. Stance on shoulder of Holtanna itself. 3rd pitch is easy climbing to the top.

Return: Two short rappels with firm anchors past the hole and down onto the col. From there you can easily move across to the entry point to Sofaruta, which we describe below.

Mohns topp to the left and Holtanna to the right. Photo: Stig J. Helset

Climbing the upper section of Sofaruta. Photo: Stig J. Helset

7.2 MOHNS TOPP SOFARUTA

Approach:	Follow the path up from the base camp by the lake, past the overnight hollow under Reiulf Steen on a distinct ridge, then traverse a steep flank along the path towards the enormous Børresteinen. Then head towards the col south of Mohns Pinnacle. Follow a narrow ledge along the wall until you come to the entry point in the south wall of Mohns topp, which is just where you catch a glimpse of the Hjørundfjord.
Length:	120 metres
Grading:	4 +
Equipment:	Helmet, climbing harness, climbing shoes, rope and a normal rack.
Description:	1st pitch goes up a marked and fast firm solid dihedral and continues up to the right to the lofty stance Sofaen. 2nd pitch starts with a short diagonal traverse down three metres towards the right, before reaching easier climbing terrain up along the face of the south wall. Take a stance on the fore-summit to avoid rope pull. 3rd pitch is short, but steep and airy.
Return:	Easy climbing down the north ridge and hike down the Mohnsrenna gully to Børresteinen and the base camp.

Climbing in the lofty top crack on Sørvestegga/Snickers. Photo: Eirik Vaage

JØNSHORNET,
THE WESTERN PART OF THE SOUTH FACE

Here we describe two great routes on the south face of the highest mountain in Molladalen. The approach and return are the same for both: follow the path up from the campsite beside Storevat-net, past the overnight hollow under Reiulf Steen on a distinct ridge and continue straight up to the right of the Jønshornrenna gully.

7.3 SØRVESTEGGA

Length: 200 metres
Grading: 5 +
First ascent: Iver Gjelstenli, Tore Lundberg and Bjørn M. Øverås 1980.
Equipment: Helmet, climbing harness, climbing shoes, two ropes and a normal rack and in addition a
              plentiful supply of friends.
Description: 1st pitch goes up a zig-zag dihedral immediately below the Sørvestegga ridge and offers
              great laid-back climbing. Stance when you reach the ridge itself. The next four pitches
              roughly follow the ridge with varied and enjoyable chimney climbing (if you stretch the
              rope lengths, you can manage with three).
Return: Here you have two alternatives: a) Two rappels with firm anchors down the west face to
              the Jønshornrenna gully and then a hike down the gully to the base camp. B) one rappel
              down the west face, then traverse out onto the Sørvestegga ridge and two rappels down
              the ridge back to the entry point.

South face of Jønshornet. Sørvestegga to the left. Snickers to the right. Photo: Stig J. Helset

Climbing in the top crack on Sørvestegga/Snickers. Holtanna in the background. Photo: Eirik Vaage

7.4 SNICKERS

Length: 200 metres
Grading: 6
First ascent: To Osten: Ole Haltvik and Tore Lundberg 1989.
                To the top: Jon Hagen and Helge Standal 1989.
Equipment: Helmet, climbing harness, climbing shoes, two ropes and a normal rack.
Description: The entry point is to the right of the entry point on the Sørvestegga, roughly in the centre
                of the western section of the south wall. 1st pitch goes straight up dihedral and crack
                formations, before you swing to the left and take stance on a large ledge, grade 5 +. 2nd
                pitch goes up to a new ledge, immediately below a distinct dihedral, grade 5 +. Take
                stance here. 3rd pitch starts with a small traverse out onto the gallery to the right, before
                moving steeply up in wonderful dihedrals, grade 6. Maximise the rope length and take
                a stance almost on the Sørvestegga ridge, just above Osten, which is an enormous block.
                4th pitch starts with a traverse round a corner to the right, before you go up a dihedral to
                the Sørvestegga ridge. From here you can either follow the ridge to the summit, grade 5 -,
                or climb up a little before traversing out to the right to the lofty top crack and climb this
                straight up, grade 5+.

A steep strenuous ascent on Snickers. Photo: Eirik Vaage

From the start of the 3rd pitch and the crux on Snickers. Holtanna in the background.
Photo: Stig J. Helset

7.5   KATARSISS

Length: 180 metres

Grading: 7 -

First ascent: Helge Standal and Kjetil Solbakken 1987/1989. The offwidth-crack at the top was free-
               climbed by Øyvind Festø and Åsmund Vaage in 2003.

Equipment: Helmet, climbing harness, climbing shoes, two ropes, a normal rack and a couple of large
               camalots.

Description: 1st pitch goes up the perfect second crack from the right, grade 6. Stance on a good ledge.
               2nd pitch goes first up to a thin slab, then diagonally to the right towards the start of the
               long dihedral, grade 7 -. Stance on first fore-summit. 3rd pitch with an easy start across to
               the next wall and then steeply up a distinct dihedral, grade 6. Stance below the top wall.
               4th pitch goes up dihedral formations and finishes with an off-width crack out to the right
               on the top wall, grade 7 -.

Return: Three rappels with solid anchors down the south wall itself.

KRUTTÅRNET

We describe two great routes on the south wall of this fantastic rock formation. Approach and return are the same for both: follow the path up from the campsite beside Storevatnet, past the overnight hollow under Reiulf Steen on a distinct ridge, then traverse on a steep flank along the path towards Børresteinen. Then go straight up and keep to the left below the pinnacle H-3-needle and down into the gully west of it. Continue on up towards the left to the entry point at the foot of Kruttårnet.

Climbing in the second S-crack on Iriss.
Photo: Stig J. Helset

7.6   IRISS

Length: 180 metres
Grading: 6 +
First ascent: Tore Lundberg and Helge Standal 1986.
Equipment: Helmet, climbing harness, climbing shoes, two ropes, a normal rack and some extra
                 medium-sized friends and small hexes.
Description: 1st pitch goes up the perfect first crack to the right, grade 6. Stance on a good ledge. 2nd
                 pitch goes first up two steep dihedrals and on up the first S-crack, grade 6 +. Stance on a
                 small ledge. 3rd pitch goes up to the first fore-summit and over into a simple transport to
                 the next wall. Stance here. 4th pitch goes up the second S-crack, grade 6. Stance below
                 the top wall. 5th pitch goes up the left-hand section of the top wall. You can also choose to
                 climb the more challenging last pitch described under Katarsiss.

Kruttårnet. Katariss to the left. Iriss to the right. Photo: Helge Standal

8 SPORTS CLIMBING AND BOULDERING

There are many well-established sport climbing areas around the coast of Sunnmøre. The area offers everything from easy slab climbing to overhanging walls, from 10 metres and up to three pitches. The best crags are to be found overlooking the Austefjord in Volda and not least on the sea-cliffs out on the coastal islands. The selection below includes three crags and a couple of the best bouldering fields in the region.

Bouldering on Godøya with an ocean view. Photo: Eirik Vaage

8.1 AUSTEFJORDEN
NEDSTEFELTET (THE LOWER FIELD)

Approach: Follow the E39 (from September 2012) from the centre of Volda through the Rotsethorn tunnel and then the Hjartå tunnel for about 10 km along the east side of the Austefjord. Park at a lay-by 100 metres after you leave the second tunnel. Follow the well defined path down and to the left of the lay-by for about 5 minutes, which brings you to the entry point.

Equipment: Helmet, harness, climbing shoes, rope and a normal rack.

Description: The main wall is about 45 metres high and offers a large number of great slab routes, graded from 4 to 7. It is easy to rig a top anchor or rappel anchor in large pine trees and expansion bolts at the top, which can be reached by walking and scrambling along the path that goes straight down from the lay-by. Take great care to avoid stumbling over the edge! The west wall is about 20 metres high and offers steeper routes, partly in cracks. This is mostly traditional climbing, with grades from 6 to 8. Rappel anchor at the top of all the routes here.

Nedstefeltet above the Austefjord. Photo topos: Tommy Skeide

Climbing on the left-hand section of Nedstefeltet.
Photo: Eirik Vaage

8.2 VALDERØYA

DAUDMANNSHELLAREN AND HELLARHYLLA

Approach:

Alternative 1: Daudmannshellaren: Turn right at the roundabout just before the centre of Ålesund and drive down into the undersea tunnel system on the RV658 in the direction of Vigra/ Giske/Godøya. After leaving the second tunnel, you are on the island of Valderøya. Turn left at the first junction after 300 metres, and then immediately right at the roundabout. Continue for 800 metres – under the main road – as far as the clubhouse belonging to Valdervoll IL, where you park the car. Walk a further 200 metres along a gravel track and turn right onto a path. Follow this until you reach a scree slope, and head for the distinct overhang at the end of the field. You are now at the entry to the Daudmannshellaren ledge, which is the lowest part of the wall. The Hellarhylla ledge lies immediately above Daudmannshellaren and is visible as a lighter-coloured vertical face – about 20 metres high and 100 metres across. To get onto the ledge you have to approach from the left as seen from below.

Alternative 2: Hellarhylla: Follow the same gravel track as to Daudmannshellaren, but this time walk 400 metres from the clubhouse at Valdervoll. Then turn right and walk for about 70 me-

Daudmannshellaren on the island of Valderøya.
Photo topos: Tommy Skeide

tres along a path signposted to Skjonghellaren, up to a small plateau with juniper bushes, and then break off to the right when you see the hint of a path. Keep to the right of wet terrain and follow the right-hand edge of the rock field for about 60 metres. There you turn right on a well defined path in slightly steeper terrain. Follow this path for about 150 metres, until you are up on the Hellarhylla ledge. The rock face is round the corner and not visible from the field.

Equipment: Helmet, harness, climbing shoes, rope and a normal rack.

Description: Valderøya has a steep smooth west-facing cliff face that is clearly visible to everyone driving to the airport on the island of Vigra. Several climbing walls lie spread along the west side of the island, but here we only include two of the most well-known cliffs. At the bottom lies Daudmannshellaren – a ledge which is passed daily by visitors to the more famous Skjonghellaren. The climbing here is overhanging and steep, but the rock has been sculptured and eroded by the waves that once broke against this former cliff-face. As an upper balcony to Daudmannshellaren lies Hellarhylla. The rock-face here is vertical, and this time it is the wind and rain that has eroded and sculpted the rock. There are some easy routes on Daudmannshellaren, but even more easy routes up on Hellarhylla. Both walls have a number of routes of varying difficulty. You can still climb on Daudmannshellaren in wet weather, but Hellarhylla certainly offers the best views. Small barbecue hearths have been established at the foot of the cliffs, so all you need to enjoy a special meal is charcoal, a grate and some tasty food. If you want to stay the night, Daudmannshellaren will double as a bivouac. There is room to sit and shelter from the rain, but remember to take some water with you!

Hellarhylla on the island of Valderøya
Photo topos: Tommy Skeide

A steep ascent on Daudmannshellaren. Photo: Tommy Skeide

8.3　NERLANDSØYA MULEVIKA

Approach:　Follow the E39 from Ørsta or Volda and turn off towards Ulsteinvik at a large roundabout, through two tunnels and a long undersea tunnel. Follow the RV653 towards Ulsteinvik, but a few kilometres after emerging from the deep tunnel, turn off left onto the RV654 towards Fosnavåg. Follow the RV654 past Fosnavåg out to the island of Nerlandsøya. Follow the signs to Kvalsvika and drive right across the island until you come to the car park at the end of the road. From here you will see a magnificent sandy beach. Make for the beach, before heading up to a cliff that you can see on the left.

Equipment:　Helmet, harness, climbing shoes, rope and a normal rack.

Description:　The climbing area is one of the most perfect in the whole of Sunnmøre, with a large number of shorter and longer routes on solid rock with good texture. Some of the routes rely on wedges, but most of them are bolted, and their difficulty ranges from 3 to 8. The view of to sea is wonderful all the time, and it is great to camp at the foot of the cliffs.

Mulevika. Left-hand section. Photo topos: Tommy Skeide

Climbing in the left-hand section of the field in Mulevika. Muletua in the background. Photo: Stig J. Helset

Mulevika, right-hand section. Photo topos: Tommy Skeide

8.4   VIGRA BOULDERING

Approach: Turn right at the roundabout just before the centre of Ålesund and drive down into the undersea tunnel system on the RV658 in the direction of Vigra/Giske/Godøya. After leaving the second tunnel, you are on the island of Valderøya. Head in the direction of the airport until you cross the small bridge between Valderøya and Vigra. Instead of turning left in towards the airport, keep straight ahead on the FV137 and through the underpass under the runway. 700 metres later you come to a junction where you turn right towards Roald. After 1.3 km you are right between the jetties in the centre of Roald, where you turn left onto a road that bends back in the same direction you have come from. Turn right at the first junction and drive to the end of the road. Now you can see Budafjellet immediately in front of you. Continue on foot on the same road you drove along, which gradually becomes a short farm track. Then follow a well defined path over a rise that separates Budafjellet from the slightly higher Molnesfjellet to the left. Go along the right-hand edge of the rise, and climb over a gate on the track. The whole walking distance is about 500 metres. Look for the brick bunker that marks the start of climbing field.

Equipment: Climbing shoes, chalk bag and crash pad.

Description: Way out by the Norwegian Sea as neighbour lie a number of cliffs and boulders that have been sculpted by nature over thousands of years. Now they are handled by climbers. The field has something that the boulder fields at Flø and Sula lack: plenty of simple, inviting challenges concentrated in a tiny area. As such this field is ideal for beginners and a great place to take your children for their first taste of climbing outdoors. Out here the small walls and boulders lie close together – it is never more than 100 metres between the extremes. The climbing takes place round a large mound that was used as a fortress by the German soldiers occupying the area during the Second World War. You can see the characteristic grey concrete walls of the bunker on the south side of the mound. On the north side and below the field the waves wash over the rocks, and the sea stretches out until it becomes just a thin line on the distant horizon. A few hundred metres further west lies a beautiful sandy beach that is perfect for bathing. Here and there the elements have eroded great holes in the boulders, making the holds in the overhangs much easier. The good holds mean that your body strength and the ability to "put your foot down" at the top are just as important as the strength of your fingers. Some of the less steep walls lack the good jugs, thus offering the excitement and challenge of balance climbing. The field has a great deal of fun climbing, but if you are looking for really difficult routes, you are in the wrong place. In the winter this is the first place where the snow melts, and the rock soon warms in the pale February sun. It is possible to find routes that are sheltered from the wind, so it is no problem climbing here whether there is a biting north-easterly or a raw south-westerly. The landings are mostly on soft grass or heather, but even so we recommend a crash pad, since most of the boulders are about 3 metres high.

Bouldering on the island of Vigra. Photo: Tommy Skeide

Clean lines on big boulders. Photo Eirik Vaage

8.5   FLØ BOULDERING

Approach: Follow the E39 from Ørsta or Volda and turn off towards Ulsteinvik at a large rounda-
              bout, through two tunnels and a long undersea tunnel. Follow the RV653 to the centre of
              Ulsteinvik, and then follow the signs to Flø. From Ålesund you can take the E136, E39 and
              the RV61 to the ferry from Sulesund-Hareid. Keep on the RV61 to Ulsteinvik and then fol-
              low the signposts to Flø. Drive to the end of the road, until you come to a No Entry sign,
              and park beside a small building. Then walk the last couple of kilometres along a good
              gravel road towards the open sea. At the end of that road you will find the first boulders.

Equipment: Climbing shoes, chalk bag and crash pad.

Description: Flø offers wonderful sport in a blockfield with an endless number of huge rocks and
              boulders that lie scattered across a beautiful rural landscape right on the coast. There are
              several factors that make Flø a must for anyone interested in bouldering. The quality of
              the rock is incredibly good, and since it is on the coast, the friction is usually excellent.
              You find overhanging boulders, vertical boulders, slabs, high boulders and low boulders,
              and what has been established so far has good, flat landings. We still recommend crash
              pads on a number of the boulders since they can be up to four metres high.

              Flø offers plenty of good climbing for beginners, but there is also more than enough to
              challenge more experienced climbers, with several boulders in category 7. But the field is
              large, and without a doubt there are still plenty of interesting bouldering problems wai-
              ting to be discovered. If you fancy bouldering in spectacular Sunnmøre scenery with the
              fresh sea breeze in your face, you should certainly pay a visit to Flø. The view of the sea
              really adds a special dimension, and it is great to camp among the boulders. For comforta-
              ble accommodation, we can recommend the cabins at Flø Feriesenter.

Bouldering at Flo. Photo: Sindre Dimmen

Bouldering in the indoor climbing silo in Volda. Photo: Olav Standal Tangen

VOLDA KLATRESILOEN

This is a former silage silo that has been converted into an 11-metre high climbing wall. The silo stands right beside a red barn just west of the University College. You can find varied climbing from grade 3 to 8 on a vertical wall via slight overhang to a roof overhang, and in addition there is also a bouldering wall that can be raised and lowered, with a fatass underneath. During opening hours, anyone is welcome to climb there for a small fee. Clubs, groups and organisations can also hire the hall.
See the website: www.skk-nytt.com

ULSTEINVIK KLIVREHALLEN

Klivrehallen is a silo in a red barn at Osneset that Klivrelaget has been converted into a climbing wall. It is 10 metres high with a floor area of 4 x 5 metres. Every inch of space has been used and there are about 180 square metres of climbing surface in the hall, offering 15-20 routes varying in difficulty from grade 3 to 8. In addition there is a motorised bouldering wall that can be raised and lowered to give the perfect opportunity for systematic bouldering training. There is a fatass beneath the wall. During opening hours, anyone is welcome to climb there for a small fee. Clubs, groups and organisations can also hire the hall. For further information about opening hours, prices and the like,
see the website: www.klivrelaget.com

ÅLESUND SUNNMØRSHALLEN

This is the largest climbing wall in Sunnmøre, with a maximum height of 25 metres. The hall is situated in the ColorLine Football Stadium, east of the town centre. The wall offers both overhanging and vertical climbing. Grades vary from 4 to 9. You can do both top-roping and lead-climbing. During opening hours, anyone is welcome to climb there for a small fee. For further information about opening hours, prices and the like, see the website: www.sunnmorshallen.no

Cycling a scenic route on a gravel road. Romedalstinden in the background. Photo: Espen Faugstad

9   SCENIC BIKE ROUTES

During the last twenty years the interest in cycling has increased considerably in Sunnmøre, just as in the rest of the country. Below we describe a few round trips on specially selected routes both off the beaten track and on the open road that we believe you will really enjoy on your bike. The terrain is great and the views are spectacular on all these routes, but naturally there are numerous other wonderful rides around Sunnmøre that are exciting to explore on your own initiative.

9.1   FOLLESTADDALEN AND ROMEDALEN

Approximately 19 km one way.
Return the same way or over to Vallasætra summer pasture.
Tarmac and gravel road.

Start at Hotell Ivar Aasen in the centre of Ørsta. Follow the RV655 east in the direction of Sæbø for about 4 km until you come to the bridge at Høgebrua. Do not cross the bridge but carry on along the FV55 and cycle almost the whole length of Follestaddalen. Just before you reach Kolåsen at the end of the valley, turn off left onto the farm lane marked Romedalen. You will need to negotiate a few hills to begin with, before the track flattens out and winds its way alongside the magnificent river all the way up to the Steinstøylen seter, about 7 km up the valley. On both sides of the valley you are surrounded by rows of spectacular peaks, with Kolåstinden, Romedalstinden and Hallehornet on your right and Kjerringa, Mannen, Sveddalstiden and Høgehornet on your left. From Steinstøylen you can continue on an 8 km path that crosses the Ørstaskaret ridge and return via Langedalen to Vallesætra and Mossætra, which are described in the next route. Be prepared to carry your bike on parts of the path. From the summer pastures it will not take you long to freewheel back down to the centre of Ørsta.

9.2 VALLASÆTRA / MOSSÆTRA

Approximately 16 km round trip.
Can be cycled in either direction.
Tarmac, gravel road and path.

Start at Hotell Ivar Aasen in the centre of Ørsta. Follow the RV655 east in the direction of Sæbø for about 1 km and then turn left up Mosmarkvegen. Follow the road almost as far as the graveyard and then turn left up Håkonsgata and on to the right up Engesetvegen. Follow this road up and east until you leave the housing estate and keep on up to the car park by the barrier. The actual farm track begins here, climbing steeply most of the way up to Vallasætra. The seter provides a good starting point for a number of great mountain hikes, such as the trip to Kjerringa described above or to the majestic Vassdalstinden. You can also cycle or hike up the Langedalen valley to the Ørstaskaret ridge and on down Romedalen, as we have described in the previous route.

Just before Vallasætra there is a bridge across to the neighbouring pasture Mossætra. Then follow the 6 km farm track down to the housing estate at Mosmarka. You can also turn right shortly before the estate, joining a more demanding off-road path through woods and rough grazing land. Either way, when you get to the bottom, take the Mosmarkvegen road and coast back down to the town centre. Most people can manage this short, but spectacular trip in about an hour.

Crossing the bridge between Vallasætra and Mosætra. Kjerringa in the background. Photo: Olav Tønnesen Helset

9.3 GURSKØYA RUNDT WITH A DETOUR TO RUNDE

Approximately 50 km.
Can be cycled in either direction.
Tarmac all the way.

Put your bike on the car and take the E39 out of Ørsta or Volda. At the large roundabout head for Ulsteinvik, through the two road tunnels and the undersea tunnel (cycling through this undersea tunnel is prohibited). Follow the RV653 from the tunnel towards Ulsteinvik , but turn left onto the RV61 at the Garnesvika junction. Park the car here. Turn right onto the RV654 after about 3 km and follow the road to Stokksund. Here you can turn off and follow the signposting to the bird island of Runde. This is a fantastic "detour" of about 45 km there and back. On the way out to the Goksøyr campsite you can stop at the Runde Environmental Centre that opened autumn 2009. This is an international research and information centre, where you among other things can see the gold and silver and other treasures recovered from the Dutch merchant sailing vessel Akerendam, which ran aground off the island of Runde in 1725. From the Goksøyr campsite on Runde it will take you a little less than an hour to walk up onto the cliffs at Rundebranden to watch the puffins and hundreds of other species that nest on this world-famous bird island. From the top you can also hike down to the Runde lighthouse, on the other side of the mountain. The lighthouse has been in operation since 1767, but in 2002 it was automated and the lighthouse keeper's cottage was converted into a self-catering cabin for the DNT (Norwegian Trekking Association) with 24 beds and a store of food. Safely back in Stokksund you can follow the spectacular RV61 towards Gjerdsvika and Gursken, and on back to Leikong and Garnesvika, where you left the car. As you cycle all the way round this island, the views are unforgettable, whether they be out to sea, around the fjord or across the exposed and barren landscape weathered by the elements.

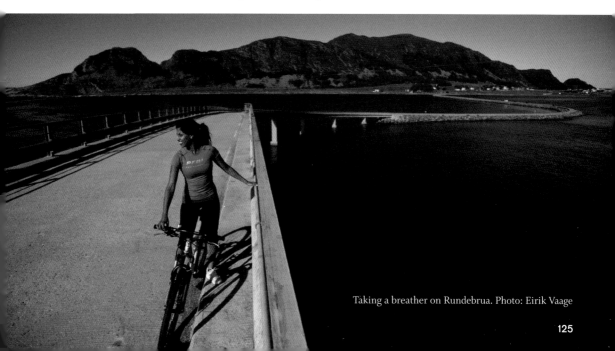

Taking a breather on Rundebrua. Photo: Eirik Vaage

9.4   ØRSTA / NORANGSDALEN / GEIRANGER / ÅLESUND / ØRSTA

Approximately 220 km.
Can be cycled in either direction.
Tarmac and gravel roads.

If you cycle this round trip, you will experience all the different parts of «The Golden Route» which is perhaps the finest tour you can make by car in the whole of Norway. Here you can enjoy crossing the Hjørundfjord, narrow stretches along gravel roads in Norangsdalen, the ferry trip into Geiranger, the steep climb up the hairpins of Ørnesvingane and the exhilarating and airy freewheeling down the hairpins of Trollstigen, as well as bumping over the cobbles in the streets of the Art Nouveau town of Ålesund.

Start at Hotell Ivar Aasen in the centre of Ørsta. Follow the RV655 east to the centre of Sæbø, a stretch of about 25 km. Take the ferry across to Lekneset, enjoying the views of Slogen, Jakta and other spectacular peaks that tower above the fjord. From Lekneset you cycle on along the RV655 in the direction of Hellesylt, which is 30 km away. But just 8.5 km after leaving the ferry, you can treat yourself to a coffee and an ice-cream at the really magnificent Union Hotel Øye. It was originally built in 1891, and at the peak of its popularity around the turn of the last century it welcomed many a prominent European aristocrat and a long list of famous pioneer climbers. There are plans to open a large new extension in the near future, from which time the hotel will be open all year round. Now cycle on up the valley. Do stop at the lake called Lygnstøylvatnet and study the foundations of the summer farm beneath the water. On 26 May 1908 a huge fall of rocks crashed down from the neighbouring peak known as Keipen and dammed up the river that runs through the valley, so that the old farm was left under water in the lake that was formed. We are pretty certain that there is not a cyclist anywhere who will not be fascinated by the incredible experience of cycling up through the vivid green landscape of this quite unique valley with its almost vertical black rock faces stretching up to the sky on both sides of the narrow, twisting road. Soon after the terrain opens up at the other end of Norangsdalen, you will find the exotic Villa Norangdal hotel on the hillside up to the right. Do go up to the hotel and sample a tasty beer from the local brewery «Slogen» while you gaze across at the magnificent Kvitegga (1717m), the highest peak in the Sunnmøre Alps outside of the Tafjordfjella area. Continue along the RV655 until you come to the junction with the RV60. Turn left and follow the signs to Hellesylt. Join the tourist ferry as it steams up the world-famous Geirangerfjord (UNESCO World Heritage site) and wonder at the spectacle of the Seven Sisters waterfalls and the mountain farms of Knivsflå and Skageflå that nestle on narrow rock ledges way up on the almost perpendicular mountainsides that surround the fjord. Embarking at the centre of Geiranger, you will join the throngs of tourists that fill the tiny village in the summer; you can visit the souvenir shops and various museums, or simply enjoy a bite to eat on the edge of the jetty. The village offers plenty of accommodation, with several first-class hotels and campsites. Geiranger is also the starting point for many easy walks or cycle trips to well-known destinations, of which Dalsnibba (1476m), a peak with a road all the way to the summit, deserves special mention. In Geiranger there are also many guided tours on offer, as well as kayaks and boats for hire, which among other things you can use to reach the foot of the paths that lead steeply up to the above-mentioned mountain farms at Knivsflå and Skageflå. Follow the RV63 along the north side of the Geirangerfjord and take the Ørnevegen up to the right.

What now awaits you is a steep climb up all of 11 hairpin bends as the road winds its way up the mountain from the fjord. Take a well-deserved rest at the viewing platform beside the final bend. From here the road climbs a little more, before you reach the top, cross the watershed and you can look forward to coasting down the gentle slopes that run down to Eidsdal and a new fjord that you cross on the ferry to Linge.

From Linge you can turn right on the RV63, cycle past Valldal and up to the top of Trollstigen in Rauma, a ride of 127 km of cycling that is mainly uphill all the way. Enjoy the view from the modern viewing platform at what is one of Norway's most frequently visited beauty spots, before you freewheel down the steep hills and bends to the bottom. From there you can follow the RV136 to Åndalsnes and on over the flatter mountain pass over Ørskogsfjellet. The best and quickest route back to Ørsta goes along the E39 from Sjøholt towards Ålesund, but make sure you turn left at the junction at Valle onto the RV656 that goes to Magerholm. Cycle on along the RV60 until it joins the E39, where you turn left and head for the ferry from Solavågen to Festøya. If you wish to visit the unique Art Nouveau town of Ålesund, you can turn right at Moa and continue along the RV136 to the town centre, which means a round trip of an extra 30 km. From Festøya you can enjoy a spectacular final stage if you cycle along the Hjørundfjord towards Standal and then climb over Standaleidet to Follestaddalen, which will bring you back to the centre of Ørsta, but you can also follow the bulk of the traffic on the main E39 along the Vartdalsfjord back to Ørsta.

Cycling past the viewing platform at Ørnesvingane. The Geirangerfjord below. Photo: Eirik Vaage

Mountain biking in Volda. Photo: Trond Kupen

10   MOUNTAIN BIKING

If you are not put off by the thought of demanding climbs, Sunnmøre is a great place for mountain biking. With so many of the towns and villages surrounded by steep mountains and forests, conditions are perfect for hiking up and riding back down again on fun single-track. In Valldal there is a bike festival, while in Volda a downhill biking competition is organised every autumn. In the long-term the cycle club in Volda want to establish downhill biking with the help of a tow/ lift, but for the time being you have to get to the top by your own power. Trailriding and freeride mountain biking have an enormous potential in Sunnmøre, and we present a mere handful of the established routes in the centre of Volda and Valldal. It is up to you to discover the rest.

The majority of mountain biking in Sunnmøre takes place on trails developed by hikers. This means the riding is demanding, both up and down. Many of the trails are in frequent use by the local hikers who enjoy the fresh air and exercise. It is important to show respect when you are riding. Hikers have the right of way over cyclists, and very often people will be positive and interested in a friendly chat about both the weather and your bike's anatomy.

A sturdy mountain bike with front or dual suspension is what you need in Sunnmøre, preferably one that works well both climbing and descending. A good helmet is mandatory and many also choose to wear elbow and knee protection. Don't forget to bring a backpack with a repair kit and warm clothing suitable for the ever changing weather. In the mountains of Norway you can experience cold weather and sudden storms even in the midst of summer. Should you be unfortunate enough to damage your bike or gear, the service is fast and skilled at G-Sport in Volda and various bike shops in Ålesund. However, spare parts may be hard to come by.

10.1 SNAUDERÅSA
VOLDA

Snauderåsa is recommended for experienced trail riders who enjoy steep and challenging terrain. From the car park follow the gravel road towards Prestesætra, which is a vantage point on the third bend. Go on a little further until you reach the sign «Steinhusa». Turn left and continue for another 300 metres until you reach the sign «Sykkelsti». This is a very old hiking trail that has been repaired and renovated in recent years. You can either turn and start the descent from this sign, or you can extend this trail by continuing on up until you reach «Gamma», an old turf hut. From here you have a great starting point for a steep descent. Snauderåsa consists of steep, technical sections with a number of sharp bends. After you have crossed the road further down, the trail becomes less steep and higher speed is possible. Beware of roads that cross your path. The trail ends immediately above the yellow teacher training college in Volda.

TRAIL BIKING IN VOLDA

To get to the trailhead, follow the RV651 from the centre of Volda up to the roundabout. Take the second exit and continue for one hundred metres before taking the first left after the roundabout. Drive uphill past the hospital on your left. Turn left at Raudemyrvegen a few hundred metres further on. Continue to the end of this road. You will find a car park and a gravel road with a barrier. This is the starting point for the trails described below.

Full speed down Snauderåsa. Photo: Trond Kupen

10.2 HÅMYRA
VOLDA

Start at the car park and follow the gravel road past Prestesætra and Steinhusa, as described in the previous route. At the end of the long uphill stretch it becomes less steep and you can see a sign on the right-hand side of the road that says "Håmyra". The trail starts just on the other side of the stream. This trail is less steep than Snauderåsa and is better suited for less experienced bikers. The trail starts across wet marshland and continues into woods with more roots and rocks. When you leave the woods, continue across the gravel road and keep to the trail on the left of the stream. The trail ends immediately before the car park and gravel road where the ascent started.

Cycling down from the top of Vardehornet. Volda and the Voldsfjord in the background.
Photo: Eirik Vaage

10.3 VARDEHORNET
VOLDA

The trip up to Vardehornet is about an hour's walk from the car park at a comfortable pace. Follow the gravel road all the way up to the Dinglevatn reservoir. Here you turn left and hike or ride along the gentle ridge up towards the summit of Vardehornet, which is on the border between Volda and Ørsta and offers a great view of the whole area. This is the starting point for a fantastic long single track descent back to the centre of Volda. The trail is technically demanding with great variety. At the top there is open landscape and lots of rocks along the path. Further down there is a short steep drop before you enter the pine forest. In the forest there are lots of roots and rocks that make it technically difficult. In addition there are relatively narrow lines between some of the trees. When you leave the woods, you can turn right and join Snauderåsa as described above. Vardehornet is a classic that offers everything a mountain biker can ever dream about.

Downhill from the top of Meljellet. Photo: Christian Nørstebo

10.4   MEFJELLET (1100 m)
VALLDAL

The wonderful trails from Mefjellet deserve much of the honour for Fjøra having become such a well-known name to all Norwegian mountain bike enthusiasts, and for why visitors from way outside our borders dream about single track descents from mountain peaks in Sunnmøre. The trip via Bjorstadnakken and Syltefjellet is a gem of a ride offering great variety.

The ride up from Fjøra starts on a road and it is possible to park at Hauge (400m). However, since the descent ends right at the fjord, you will have to climb back up after the ride to pick up your car. From Hauge continue on the gravel road to Nysætra (750m). From Nysætra the ride follows the single track up to the summit of Mefjellet. The ascent is so steep and technically difficult that for most people the only option is pushing or carrying the bike. The climb to the top of Mefjellet takes 1-2 hours, depending on where you start and how fit you are.

The first part of the descent follows the same route as you came up. The trail along the ridge offers fantastic riding. It is technical and demanding, but for skilled bikers it is all rideable. Way down below you can see the fjord. Just before the end of the ridge, turn sharply to the right. Follow the trail going northeast below the ridge you just came down. Here the single track is flat and straightforward. Most of the route is easy to navigate as far as Bjorstadnakken, where the trail turns downhill again. From here down towards Rugga the terrain is extremely steep and it can be difficult to find the trail. Once safely down you will find the hiking trail to Rugga again. Turn right at the first junction you come to. From Rugga there is a nice singletrack. Keep right at the next junction and follow the ridge and the signs to Ytterlinakken. From here it climbs 60 metres up to Syltefjellet, before you follow a fun trail down through the pine forest. At the junction after crossing the marshland you keep left, through a gate and move on along a rough track to the edge of a field. Here you make a sharp left turn and negotiate the final bends down to the farm called Ruset (350m). From here an ancient hand-built packhorse track leads you on down. This section is the first trail the local mountain bike enthusiasts discovered. It has sharp hairpin bends and several demanding but fun sections. When you reach the tarmac, turn left to get back to Fjøra.

CYCLING IN THE VALLDAL AREA

To get to the trailhead from Ålesund, follow the E136 to Moa, where you join the E39 in the direction of Trondheim/Åndalsnes. From Ørsta you follow the E39 north to the ferry Festøya-Solevågen. Stay on the E39 from Solevågen in the direction of Trondheim/Åndalsnes but at Sjøholt turn right onto the RV650 towards Geiranger. Drive through the centre of Stordal, across the mountains via Liabygda and on to the centre of Valldal, Sylte. Fjøra is about another 10 minutes' drive further up the fjord from there.

A quieter stretch above the Syltefjord. Photo: Christian Nørstebø

10.5 VARDEFJELLET (893 m)
VALLDAL

Vardefjellet is yet another little gem at Sylte. To get to the trailhead, drive up to the western end of Syltebygda, towards Lingås. If you have two cars, this trail is perfect for shuttling. Park one car at the road barrier at Lingås (300m), while the rest drive on up to Klovsetsætra summer pasture at 550m. From there you have to push your bike up a steep hill. Turn left at the trail junction and on up to Vardevatnet lake at 850m. Now those who want can test their strength at about a kilometre of enjoyable uphill pedalling. Allow the best part of an hour to get to the top. The summit is open and impressive, and after you have lowered the seat and made sure your helmet is fastened properly, you are ready to warm up on the first downhill stage to the lake and slightly beyond it. The rest of the descent is fun and more technical. There are no dangerous points and no particularly difficult sections, but the trail still offers challenges all the way down. You have to be alert all the time to guarantee a smooth ride. In particular a couple of traverses, a stream and several hairpin bends will keep you on your toes. If you are at your best, pushing hard and keeping the flow going down this stretch is really cool! Safely down at Klovsetsætra you can get your breath back with a brief stop at this seter, before picking up the trail again at the bottom of the meadow. Ride a short stretch on the gravel road before taking the ancient hand-built packhorse track, which winds its way down the hillside. Cross the road once more, and stop down by the road barrier at Lingås.

10.6 ANSOKHORNET (888 m)
LIABYGDA

Ansokhornet allows you to do much of the ascent by car and offers a wonderful descent that ends on the ferry quay in Liabygda. If you dare to trust yourself, your bike and the tyres, you may be able to ride down steeper trails than you have ever descended before.

The trip up from Liabygda starts on the road. The upper car park is 300m above the farm called Ansok. From here you keep straight and cycle along the farm track for a few hundred metres and through a gate. From the top of the hill you follow the trail to the right. Next is 400mH of uphill pushing. As a mountain biker it is natural to turn around at a vantage point some way below the actual summit, since there are no more trails further up. Allow 1-2 hours to the turning point, depending on where you start and how fit you are.

On the descent there is plenty of good riding and a couple of technically demanding sections. Part of the trail goes along a steep precipice, and there is a dangerous section of about 20 metres where you do not want to fall off on your right-hand side. Once back at the Ansok farm the route continues past the farmhouse and across the field. Avoid damaging more grass than absolutely necessary. At the end of the field you ride under an aerial cable for transporting hay before taking a sharp left. After a couple of sharp bends you pass under the cable yet again. Now you are facing a very steep and difficult section. The descent down the rest of the hillside makes use of an ancient packhorse track until you reach the road. Here you must turn right across a field and pass straight through an old farmyard, before picking up the trail again at the bottom left-hand corner of the field. Then follow the trail until it ends in a steep set of steps, where many will prefer to get off their bikes. You will soon find yourself back on the jetty by the ferry. If you did not leave a car here, you will have to cycle up the tarmac road and through the tunnel to get back to Ansok.

10.7 LIAHORNET (961 m)
LIABYGDA

Liahornet offers the complete mountain bike experience, with steep and rocky mountain biking along with amazing views from the top and a wonderful trail through birch and pine forest further down the mountain.

Park your car in Liabygda and cycle up the gravel road towards Liasætra. From the seter a narrow path runs up the hillside to Storskardnakken. It is an effort to drag your bike up here. Once on the ridge you follow the trail along it to the summit of Liahornet, which offers spectacular views of the fjord and the surrounding countryside. On the way up take your time to study some technical sections and assess whether you have the courage and skill to attempt cycling down again. Allow 2-3 hours to reach the summit.

From the top you start by riding down the ridge you have just climbed up, which will involve some pretty challenging mountain biking. Instead of cycling back to Storskardnakken, turn left under the power lines and ride on between the mountain birches. Next is a demanding section before you emerge into an open birch wood, which leads you to a magnificent steep pine forest, where you will have to raise the seat of your bike and pedal uphill again for about 10 minutes. Turn left alongside the lake and continue on to a small summer barn. Head out onto yet another pine ridge. Now descend briefly before crossing the stream and continuing down through the pine forest with four very distinct drainage ruts. Enthusiastic cyclists have spent time with picks and shovels making it possible for you to enjoy the ride here. After the final ditch you can let go of your brakes and be at one with the terrain instead. Here it is full speed ahead across a farm track and another pine ridge, up past the waterworks and into a beautiful pine forest before the trail finishes off down a steep hiking trail back to the main road.

Biking down through a steep pine forest. Photo: Arne Litlere

Paddling up the Hjørundfjord. Photo: Eirik Vaage

11   SEA AND FJORD PADDLING

The Sunnmøre fjord landscape is well known to most people. By getting into a kayak and paddling up one of the fjords in the region, you become really close to the elements and experience a very special perspective on the scenery of Sunnmøre. A kayak can also be a very appropriate form of transport when you wish to gain access to routes for hiking and skiing that otherwise would be difficult to approach. Below we describe paddling on three of the most well known fjords in the region, in addition to a trip around the skerries further out on the coast.

11.1   HJØRUNDFJORDEN

Approach: Follow the RV655 from the centre of Ørsta towards Sæbø. Turn right over the bridge at Hustadbrua on the left-hand bend just before the centre of Sæbø, and follow the road on out towards the headland at Hustadneset. Launch your kayak wherever you find suitable.

Description: The Hjørundfjord is one of the most beautiful fjords in the world. On a calm day the mountains are reflected in the water and the whole landscape seems unreal. A recommended route can be to paddle below Skårasalen to the roadless hamlet of Skår and then cross to the other side towards Jakta, before entering the Norangsfjord. The distance across the Hjørundfjord is about 2000 metres. At the head of the Norangsfjord you find the village of Øye and Hotel Union. On the way back you can head towards the roadless hamlet of Trandal further west on the Hjørundfjord, and perhaps allow time to go ashore and pay a visit to the unusual and very original eatery Christian Gaard, before paddling across the fjord to Standal and on back to the centre of Sæbø. When you are paddling on the Hjørundfjord, you need to be aware of the danger of sudden, squally gusts of wind that rush down from the mountains and hanging valleys.

11.2   AUSTEFJORDEN

Approach: Follow the E39 (after September 2012) from the centre of Volda, the Rotsethorn tunnel and then the Hjartå tunnel on the east side of the Austefjord until you reach Fyrde. Park by the church and launch your kayak.

Description: The Austefjord is underestimated by many, and not least for paddlers it offers many fantastic outdoor experiences. The mountains on either side of the fjord are not as alpine in form as those by the Hjørundfjord, but on the other hand you can enjoy the serenity of paddling slowly down this idyllic fjord surrounded by lush green hillsides and snow-covered peaks. What is more, you will find a magnificent spot for outdoor recreation on the abandoned island of Årsetøya. Along the fjord you will also find several excellent crags for rock climbing, and on some of them you can even start climbing straight out of the kayak.

The paddler has found some unusually calm water on the Hjørundfjord.
Slogen in the background. Photo: Eirik Vaage.

11.3 GEIRANGERFJORDEN

Approach: From Ørsta you follow the RV655 to Sæbø. Take the Sæbø-Lekneset ferry and continue on the road up the Norangsdal. When you come to the RV60, turn left and drive down to the centre of Hellesylt. Here you can launch your kayak, paddle a short distance down the Storfjord before crossing to enter the Geirangerfjord.

Description: The Geirangerfjord with its World Heritage status is one of Norway's tourist destinations that can boast the most overseas visitors, and there is no better way to experience this world-famous fjord than to paddle it. On the journey in you can go ashore at several abandoned farms. You can make a stop at the open farm Matvika, which lies right on the edge of the water, just after you enter the fjord. Further in you will be surrounded by ever steeper mountainsides and the spectacular waterfall The Seven Sisters. You can also go ashore and climb the steep paths up to the abandoned mountain farms at Knivsflå and Skageflå, which cling to narrow ledges high up on either side of the fjord. At the head of the fjord you find the centre of Geiranger, which in the summer season is buzzing with tourists from every corner of the world. Here there are souvenir shops, museums and many hotels and guest houses. Geiranger is also the starting point for many great cycling and hiking trips.

Paddling on a narrow section of the Geirangerfjord. The Seven Sisters in the background. Photo: Andre Spica

143

The Seven Sisters are looking their best for the paddler. Photo: Andre Spica

11.4 EIKSUND–ULSTEINVIK

Approach: Follow the E39 from the centre of Volda or Ørsta. Turn off towards Ulsteinvik at the large roundabout and drive through three tunnels. When you leave the third, subsea tunnel, you cross a bridge and park by the marina on the right-hand side. Here you can launch your kayak.

Description: Paddle out through this typical western Norwegian archipelago, with islands, skerries and reefs as far as the eye can see. Round the headland at Aursnespynten and paddle through the Kjeldsund straits. Keep on under the bridge at Dragsundbru, before the island of Veøy appears on your right-hand side and you should head for the straits at Røyrasundet. After the straits the island of Kvitøy comes into sight on your left and now set your course towards the island of Flatøya, which you should pass on the inland side. Now hug the shore all the way in to the centre of Ulsteinvik. We recommend a visit to the Kaffikari cafe for a warm drink and a bite to eat, before you return to Eiksund the way you came. Of course it is quite possible to paddle on out into the open sea, but these waters demand a great deal of skill and experience of the paddler.

Paddling in the peace and quiet of the skerries. Photo: Eirik Vaage

12   KAYAKING

Activity on the rivers in Sunnmøre is on the increase all the time. The local paddling club in Volda now has about 10 active members who are frequently to be seen on the rivers in the area. In addition an international boarding school in Ørsta offers river paddling on its timetable, and the school uses the local rivers for instruction and recreation. One result of all this increased interest is that the paddling competition X-creek in the Rossåa river in Ørsta has become an annual happening for paddlers from all over the country.

Kayaking in Sunnmøre is an activity that has to be fairly spontaneous, since the water flow is very uneven. The finest period is during the snow-melting in April and May. At that time it does not take more than some sun and a temperature a few degrees above freezing point before the flow is really good. In addition the water flow is good in September and October when the heavy autumn rain showers sweep across the area. That is why it is a good idea to have your kayak on the car-roof and all the equipment in the boot. It is difficult to plan this sort of activity so you need to be ready to go whenever the conditions are good. The website www.riverflow.no analyses data continually from NVE's measuring stations (Norwegian Water Resources and Energy Directorate). This gives paddlers a useful indication of how suitable the water flow is for kayaking. Nevertheless each paddler must assess the river in relation to his or her own skills and ability. In general the rivers change a good deal after they have been in flood. Therefore it is important to survey the river first to register any trees and rocks that may have been moved since the last time you paddled the same stretch of water.

GRADING

Class 1   Fast running water with waves. No particular obstacles.
Hazards: None other than those you expect in running water.

Class 2   Water that requires some manoeuvring. Can be tiring for inexperienced paddlers.
Hazards: Can be risky if you have to swim and maybe hit rocks in the water.

Class 3   Strong currents and many turns in demanding water.
Hazards: Potential danger of hitting rocks underwater and of capsizing.

Class 4   Very strong currents, many turns and some minor waterfalls.
Hazards: High risk of hitting rocks and of capsizing.

Class 5   Very strong currents, many turns, difficult to judge flow and high waterfalls.
Hazards: Extreme risk of hitting rocks and of capsizing.

Class 6   Suitable only the most experienced paddlers.
Hazards: Simple mistakes can have fatal consequences.

Classic Sunnmøre rapids. Photo: Benjamin Hjort

12.1 ROSSÅA
ØRSTA

Grade: 3 – 4
Distance: 550 metres
Approach: Follow the RV655 from the centre of Ørsta towards Sæbø, but turn left up Mosmarkvegen after a kilometre. Turn off towards the new graveyard on the left-hand side of the road, immediately after the bridge. Look over the parapet of the bridge as you cross it. That will give you a good indication of how swelling the river is. Drive on until the tarmac gives way to a floodlit ski track and leave the car in order to study the waterfall at Jettefossen.
Description: Rossåa has everything. Waterfalls, slides, high speed, fun curves and good eddies. The river runs through the centre of Ørsta and gets its water supply from the two valleys Langedalen and Nupadalen. With this relatively small catchment area it is not surprising that the water flow in the Rossåa changes so rapidly. In the autumn it is therefore important to keep a close check on the rainfall the night before, and have all your equipment at the ready in the car. When the snow is melting in the spring, the water flow is generally good. If the water is flowing 10-15 cm over the rocks on the left of the waterfall, then conditions are perfect. Put in immediately above Jettefossen, and keep well to the right over the edge. Survey s-turns and narrow slides 100 and 250 metres below the bridge. The exit of the s-turn contains a rock where there has been a threat of pinning once or twice, so do keep your eyes open if you are heading in that direction. The take out is at the next bridge, where the RV655 runs towards Sæbø.

12.2 ØYRAELVA
VOLDA

Grade: 3 – 4
Approach: Follow the RV651 from the centre of Volda. At the roundabout take the second exit up Vikebygdvegen. 300 metres after the roundabout you turn off sharp right down Årnesvegen. Parking and put in from the lakeside recreational area at Årneset beside Rotevatnet. The take out is on the river bank to the left under the bridge – 100 metres before the river joins the fjord. When you are walking back to fetch the car, you can walk along the riverside path up the picturesque valley back to the lake.
Description: The river starts at the southern end of the lake and paddling requires high water flow in the form of rain and/or snow-melting. Spring and autumn are the best times to try your hand at «urban» river paddling in Volda. The river flows at an even pace, has few eddies and requires reconnaissance before you put in. The river runs through a wood and a built-up area. It is important to survey the river for trees and other hazards. The river starts quietly and becomes steeper and steeper and more technically demanding, the closer you get to the centre of town. Beware of shallow holes and sharp rocks. If your technique is good and you feel you are in good shape, you will certainly take several trips on this exciting stretch of water that is so close to civilisation.

Dropping in Rossåa. Photo: Sindre Dimmen

In no particular hurry on the gentle but rocky Follestaddalselva. Photo: Joar Wæhle

12.3 FOLLESTADDALSELVA
ØRSTA

Grade: 2-3

Approach: Follow the RV655 from the centre of Ørsta in the direction of Sæbø. After 4 km you come to the bridge at Høgebrua. The put in is 300 metres further up the river. The take out is at the suspension bridge or possibly at the marina in the centre of Ørsta.

Description: At Høgebrua you will get an indication of the water flow and what to expect. The river requires high water flow and is at its best during the spring snow-melting season. During periods with extremely high water, e.g. in the case of flooding, the river can present a number of challenges, and it is important to survey the hole immediately below the bridge. The hole is situated right in the middle of the river and can be extremely dangerous. In periods of very high water it is normal for beginners to start below the hole. With less water volume you have plenty of time before the hole and it is rarely a problem. In general the river offers great paddling, and is well suited for beginners. There are good eddies downriver, and the river becomes calmer as you approach the estuary and the fjord.

12.4 FYRDSELVA
AUSTEFJORDEN

Grade: 2-3

Approach: Follow the RV651/E39 from the centre of Volda through the Rotsethorn tunnel and the Hjartå tunnel and on in to Fyrde at the head of the fjord, where you will see the Fyrdselva river entering the fjord. Continue upriver and past the first lake. Park on the right-hand side of the road. The put in is immediately above a small drop of one meter. The take out is downriver from the waterfall just before the fjord.

Description: This is a river that has relatively stable water discharge and can be paddled on summer days when there is not enough water in the other rivers. The river starts with a small drop of one meter. During high water there is a certain amount of backwash in this waterfall, and you ought to take the precaution of having a throw-line. On the next reaches there are easy rapids with good eddies. Below the lake the current increases again and the trip ends with a drop of 4 metres. Surveying and protection on the right-hand bank of the river. We recommend this location for both beginners and more experienced paddlers. In this river you may be asked about disinfection. It is important that all your equipment is disinfected and that you show respect to anyone fishing here.

Full speed over the edge. Photo: Joar Wæhle

Modest rapids, but still great paddling. Photo: Joar Wæhle

12.5 BYGDAELVA
HELLESYLT

Grade: 4-5

Approach: Follow the RV655 from the centre of Ørsta to Sæbø. Take the ferry Sæbø-Lekneset and continue along the RV655 up the Norangsdal. When you reach the RV60, turn left towards Hellesylt. Drive to the centre of Hellesylt and on up the valley on the FV80. The put in is about 200 metres upriver from the powerhouse. The river is clearly visible from the road.

Description: This river is called «Race Course» since it is the perfect section of water for a downhill paddling competition. It has everything from slides and drops to technically demanding rapids. You will happily paddle this section ten times in a row. The river can be paddled even with low or medium water flow. Bygdaelva is a good alternative when there is not enough water in the other rivers. Be aware of the final drop before the powerhouse. Here it is easy to underestimate the current which flows fast in under the rocks on both the right-and left-hand sides. A throw-line is necessary. Note that it is also a requirement that your kayak has been disinfected to avoid transmitting salmon lice. Disinfectant can be purchased at Stadheimsfossen Camping & Hytter.

12.6 EIDSELVA
NORDFJORDEID

Grade: 2

Approach: From Volda you take the ferry to Folkestad and continue on the E39 (new classification after Sept 2012) towards Bergen. Turn left onto the RV15 to Stryn after the descent from Stigedalen. Immediately after the bridge at the turning to Stryn you will find the put in by the car park on the right. The take out is at the next bridge in the centre of Nordfjordeid.

Description: This is a calm and attractive river that is ideal for beginners and others who want to experience a quieter form of river paddling. After about 200 metres the river is regulated, so that portage is necessary past a powerhouse on the left bank. Below the powerhouse the river flows freely through open countryside and offers enjoyable paddling with wave-trains and large eddies on both sides of the river. The river is at its deepest and best in high water after the snow melting in the spring or after heavy rain in the autumn.

Two paragliders soaring above Saudehornet and Vassdalstinden. Photo: Vidar Larsen

13   PARAGLIDING

Paragliding has become a popular sport in the area during the last twenty-five years, and there are many easily accessible starting points for flights. The scenery and topography of this north-western corner of southern Norway mean that all the flights here are really different from anything you can experience elsewhere in Scandinavia. It is relatively simple to get a taste of what is on offer by taking a tandem-trip organised by one of the many clubs in the region.

Hazards: Paragliding is considered by many to be an extreme sport. It can also be so if you so de-
             sire, but that is against all the principles of the sport. If you respect the certificate system
             SafePro, there is little risk of accidents. As a rule it is when the pilot pushes the limits that
             accidents happen. More information is available on the website of Norsk luftsportforbund
             www.nlf.no (Norwegian Air Sport Federation).
Season: 365 days a year.

13.1 ØRSTA SKISENTER (Bondalseidet)

NB! All flights here must be reported to the control tower at the local airport, Ørsta-Volda Lufthamn tel. 70 04 16 89. Bondalseidet is the best location for paragliding in Ørsta municipality and it has been the venue for many very successful Norwegian national championships. Many long routes have been flown from the top of the ski lift at this facility: north to Barstadvika (24 km), northeast to Ørskogfjellet (52 km), east to Stryn (58 km), south to Jølstravatnet (73 km) and west to Gjerdsvika on the island of Gurskøya (41 km).

Approach:	Drive 15 km from the centre of Ørsta towards Sæbø on the RV655. Turn left at the signpost marked «Skisenter».
Open:	In the winter the chair lift is open every Saturday and Sunday from 10-16.
Price:	NOK 40 on the chairlift to the summit.
Elevation:	About 700 m.
Wind:	Northwest via south to northeast depending on which starting point is chosen.
Hazards:	Light thermals in northwesterly wind on the south side. Power lines north of the main landing area beside the RV655.
Pilot:	Level 3. With an instructor present pilots with level 2 may also start.
GPS-start:	Point BDEIDS, easterly direction 0359007, northerly direction 6894837, Bondalseidet.

13.2   BREKKEHEIDA
ØRSTA

NB! All flights here must be reported to the control tower at the local airport, Ørsta-Volda Lufthamn tel. 70 04 16 89. Brekkeheida lies just outside the centre of Ørsta and is well-suited for flying on sunwise breeze in the summer half of the year. The location has its own windsock that is clearly visible from the town centre.

Approach:	Follow the RV655 from the centre of Ørsta towards Sæbø for about 1 km and then turn left up Mosmarkvegen. Follow the road past the graveyard and right up to the highest part of the housing estate. Park by the Swiss-style Tyrol house and follow a distinct path for just under half an hour until you reach Brekkeheida.
Elevation:	350 m.
Wind:	Only sunwise breeze.
Hazards:	When launching be aware of thermals.
Pilot:	Level 3 and above.
GPS-start:	Point BRKHD, easterly direction 0352797, northerly direction 6899392, Brekkeheida.

13.3   TURHEISEN (CHAIRLIFT) IN SPJELKAVIK
ÅLESUND

NB! All flights here must be reported to the control tower at Ålesund airport, Vigra tel. 67 03 54 71. This is the regional airport. The local Ålesund club have the chairlift at their disposal since they contribute actively to its operations. On 20.06.2010 a flight of over 18 km was made from this starting point.

Approach:	From Ålesund you take the E136 to Moa and the centre of Spjelkavik. From Ørsta you follow the E39 to the ferry Festøya-Solevågen and then on to Moa and the centre of Spjelkavik. From the centre you turn off east and follow the signposts to the chairlift.
Open:	The chairlift operates every Sunday during the summer half of the year from 10.30-16.30 if the weather is suitable for flying. The lift is open if the flag is flying from the summit. If not, it takes about half an hour to walk up the line of the lift.
Price:	NOK 50.
Wind:	Flying in wind directions NE-N-NW.
Start height:	350 m.
Restrictions:	Maximum 2500 feet west and north of the chairlift, and 3500 feet east and south of the lift.
Landing:	Main landing area east of the football pitch.
Hazards:	None in particular.
GPS-start:	N 62°27 ' 12" E 6°21' 12"

Acro flying. Photo: Anders Crook

VOLDA/ØRSTA HIMMELSEGLARLAG

Volda/Ørsta Himmelseglarlag was founded in 1978 and today has about 40 members. The club welcomes guests and tandem fliers and also has a clubhouse where visitors are welcome to stay the night. On their website you will also find the coordinates for various flying venues: www. himmelseglarane.com

Flying above the centre of Stranda. The Storfjord in the background. Photo: Hans Kristian Krogh-Hanssen

13.4 SULAFJELLET
LANGEVÅG

NB! All flights here must be reported to the control tower at Ålesund airport, Vigra tel. 67 03 54 71. This is a 12 km long mountain ridge launch location south of Ålesund. On 26.05.2010 a flight of over 26 km was made from this starting point.

Approach: Follow the E39 from Ålesund or Ørsta (including a ferry crossing to Solavågen), and then the RV61 and RV657 to Langevåg. Ask the way to Kummen, the old dam used by the local waterworks. Drive past the main landing area on your way to Kummen. Walk up the pipeline and turn right at the top, which will bring you to the start, a walk of about 40 minutes from the car park.

Wind: The prevailing wind is NW-N-NE, usually with a forecast of 4-5 m/s.

Restrictions: 2500 feet.

Landing: Along the whole length of the ridge.

Hazards: Shooting range east of the start. Do not fly over this if the red flag is flying!

GPS-start: N 62°25 ' 27" E 6°11' 27"

ÅLESUND HANG- AND PARAGLIDER CLUB

Ålesund Hang Glider Club was founded in 1975. At that time it was purely a hang glider club. When paragliding was introduced as a sport towards the end of the 1980s, several members started that activity, and the club changed its name to Ålesund Hang- and Paraglider Club, which is still its official name to this day, even though there are no longer any active hang glider pilots. The club has today about 40 members, of whom roughly half are quite active. On the club's website www.aapgk.net you can find further information about the area.

13.5 STRANDA SKISENTER

NB! All flights here must be reported to the control tower at Ålesund airport, Vigra tel. 67 03 54 71.

Approach:	From Ørsta you can drive north on the E39 to Festøya. Take the ferry to Hundeidvik, and follow the signs to Stranda. Do not cross the large bridge at Ikkornes/Sykkylven, but keep straight ahead at the roundabout, which will save you an expensive toll charge. On your way to the town centre of Stranda, you cannot miss the ski area Stranda Skisenter. From Ålesund you can drive north on the E39 and take the Magerholm-Sykkylven ferry before heading on to Stranda Ski Resort.
Open:	Today the ski lift facilities are only open during the winter, but the plan is that the ski resort will be open all the year round from the summer of 2012.
Wind:	Flying is possible with all wind directions.
Elevation:	950m if you walk from the top of the ski lift up to the highest point on the Langedalsegga ridge. On Roaldshornet (1230m) side there is a height difference of about 800 metres in the ski lift facility.
Hazards:	The ski lift facility.
GPS-start:	N 62°18 ' 31" E 6°50' 42" on the Roaldshorn mountain ski lift.

Paraglider hovering above Breisundet and Godøya. Photo: Torstein Støylen

Colourful clefts and spectacular underwater landscapes characterise scuba diving in Sunnmøre. Photo: Lill Haugen

14   SCUBA DIVING

Scuba diving in Sunnmøre can provide you with experiences on a par with the best in the world, and both Norwegian Championships and World Championships in underwater photography have been organised in this area. Aegir Scuba Diving Club has on a number of occasions organised Norwegian National Championships in underwater hunting and in addition the Nordic Championships in 2005. Underwater life in the area is greatly influenced by the Gulf Stream, which flows north along the coast just off the West Cape. This current is the source of huge areas covered by kelp forests, an amazing underwater world teeming with life and plenty of currents between inlets and islands. The rugged coastal landscape has led to many shipwrecks down through history. Also, there are some exciting wrecks from the Second World War here which attract divers from both home and abroad.

In the autumn huge quantities of herring seek refuge in the fjords from the seasonal storms. Flocks of killer whales and pilot whales follow these herring schools along the coast and into the fjords. If your luck is in and you are in the right place at the right time, you will have the chance to see these magnificent creatures on one of your diving trips. If you travel out to Runde, you will also get a teeming bird life into the bargain. The bird island of Runde is where a whole range of rare species migrate to breed, species such as sea eagle, golden eagle, marsh harrier, gyr falcon, turtle dove, hoopoe, alpine swift, eagle owl, puffin and many many more.

For further tips about diving in the area, contact Aegir Scuba Diving Club at www.aegir.no. Another very active club is Herøy Scuba Diving Club, which also has a compressor for filling 200 and 300 bars bottles. Herøy Scuba Diving Club also takes guests along on diving trips on its own boats. Contact the club at www.heroy-dykkarklubb.com. In Ørsta you will find Møredykk at www.moredykk.org, and Volda Scuba Diving Club is at www.dykkerklubben.com. Ålesund Sports Diving Club organise regular boat trips and have what is perhaps the finest clubhouse in Norway: www.aasdk.no. If you would rather have a purely professional programme, you can get in touch with www.dykkersenter.no in Ålesund. They organise diving trips for groups of 4 – 12 persons and run their own shop with a broad range of diving equipment.

14.1 GROTTA ON STAD

Approach: Contact Aegir for access and guiding.

Description: This is a diving experience for fine days, with diving only possible about five days a year. The dive requires a lot of planning and should be made together with the local diver on the spot. In return you are guaranteed a unique and very special experience.

Depth: 10 metres.

Certification: Basic course CMAS, PADI or equivalent, with good experience.

Seabed: Stones and rocks.

Sea life: Kelp forests, anemones and dead man's fingers.

14.2 ALNESRAUNEN

Approach: Dives at Alnesraunen must be made from a boat. Both Ålesund Sports Diving Club and Ålesund dykkarsenter organise trips to Alnesraunen when weather permits, a boat trip of less than 30 minutes from the centre of Ålesund. The islet lies facing the open sea near Godøya and fine weather is therefore essential. A swell with huge ocean rollers of 2-3 meters is not unusual in this area, so you should not dive here in poor weather.

Description: This is one of the most spectacular and well-known diving locations in Sunnmøre. Here you can experience a good catch dive or a great nature dive in kelp forests, wonderful clefts and reefs covered with anemones and dead man's fingers. Do not go deeper than 15 meters, otherwise you will miss the best clefts.

Depth: 0-15 metres.

Certification: Basic course CMAS, PADI or equivalent, with good experience.

Seabed: Wonderful kelp forests with exciting reefs and colourful clefts.

Sea life: Shoals of saithe, flatfish, sea scorpions, crabs, anemones, dead man's fingers, moss animals and lots of tiny creatures in the kelp forest.

Lush kelp forest and the deep blue of the ocean at Alnesraunen. Photo: Lill Haugen

Two totally different worlds. The old Skodjebrua in the background. Photo: Lill Haugen

14.3 SKODJESTRAUMEN

Approach: Follow the E39 from Ørsta/Ålesund and turn off towards Skodje on the RV661. Park by
                 a small, disused tunnel just after the toll booth. Walk through the tunnel and across the
                 smallest bridge and down the path to the left. Start your dive from a tiny bay, immediately
                 before the current begins. Follow the current, keeping to the left along the wall and round
                 the islet. Go ashore in the middle of the islet, where a path leads back to the road.

Description: Dives in Skodjestraumen ought to be made from a boat, but with good planning they can
                 also be made from land. This is a rapid and colourful dive. The seabed is covered with
                 dead man's fingers and waving kelp forests, and this is an exciting location for both begin-
                 ners and more experienced scuba divers.

Depth: 0-30 metres and 0-10 metres under the smallest bridge.

Certification: Basic course CMAS, PADI or equivalent.

Seabed: Sandy bottom and rock formations.

Sea life: Huge amounts of dead man's fingers, anemones, brittle stars, frilled anemones, sea cu-
                 cumbers and some catfish.

Fingers of seaweed wave to a diver beneath the bridge in the wonderful Skodjestraumen. Photo: Lill Haugen

14.4 FESTØYA

Approach: Follow the E39 from Ørsta in the direction of Ålesund. Stop immediately before the ferry
               jetty at Festøya – by a small beach at a safe distance from the ferry traffic.
Description: Start the dive from the beach and swim out from land. There is good seaweed from 0 to
               10 metres with lots of scarlet pinstripe wrasse and as a rule a good deal of nudibranchs.
               Then there is a sandy bottom with flatfish, anglerfish and some scallops. From 10 to 12
               metres you will find outcrops with dead man's fingers and beautiful vegetation, and finally
               a great wall on the right. Visibility is often good here with large shoals of saithe. Both ling
               and catfish hide in the rock formations. Do not dive deeper than you are certified to do,
               even though it can be tempting to swim further on down the wall.
Depth: 0-35 metres.
Certification: Basic course CMAS, PADI or equivalent.
Sea life: Nudibranchs, shrimp, rock gunnel, lumpsuckers, anglerfish, catfish, scallops, crabs, ling,
               cod, scarlet pinstripe wrasse and schooling fish such as herrings and poor cod.

14.5 DEN BLÅ LAGUNE

Approach: Follow the E39 from Ørsta or Volda and turn off in the direction of Ulsteinvik at the large
               roundabout, drive through two land tunnels and the long subsea tunnel. Follow the RV653
               in the direction of Ulsteinvik, but turn off onto the RV61 immediately after Haddal. Drive
               in the direction of Fosnavåg and follow the signposts to Runde. Contact Herøy Scuba
               diving Club for hire of boat and a local guide.
Description: The name Den Blå Lagune (The Blue Lagoon) originates from a combination of the
               beautiful scenery and the special colours that appear when the light is right. Here you can
               experience a nature dive with lots of fauna, clefts and potholes over a fairly large area.
Depth: 10-25 metres.
Certification: Basic course CMAS, PADI or equivalent.
GPS position: N 62°23.50' E005°36.53'.

Felix Scheder on the seabed in Åramsundet is considered one of Norway's most exciting sites for wreck diving. Photo: Lill Haugen

14.6 FELIX SCHEDER

Approach: The shipwreck of the DS Felix Scheder lies right in the middle of the ferry crossing in Åramsundet between Åram and Voksa and dives must be made from a boat. Contact Aegir Scuba Diving Club or Herøy Scuba Diving Club. There is often a strong current through the straits; diving must be made at times with no current and the ferry must always be notified that wreck dives are taking place.

The wreck: DS Felix Scheder was originally built as a whaling vessel, but was given new tasks during World War II. Under the German name V – 5307, Felix was equipped with depth charges and had two cannons mounted in the stern. On 12th September 1944 the ship was discovered by British Barracuda planes on a mission along the Norwegian coast. Under a rain of bombs the 45-metre long vessel soon sank to the depths of the ocean. 22 persons died during the attack. Felix lay alone in Åramsundet – until the wreck was visited by divers in 1984.

Description: Felix is a great wreck that lies perfectly on its keel on a white sandy seabed at a depth of 30 metres. The cannons on deck are still pointing up and southwards towards the British warplanes that appeared over the mountains. The top of the wheel house is at 22 metres deep. Broken plates lie scattered around inside the wreck. The propeller is also worth a visit. Cracks in the wreck, and in particular in the shattered machine room are good hiding places for lobster, anglerfish and catfish, and in addition smaller creatures such as rock gunnel, antler crab and edible crab. You can also often see huge ling patrolling the area round the wreck.

Depth: 25-30 metres.

Certification: CMAS***, PADI advanced or equivalent. Nitrox dive.

GPS position: N 62 122 05 E 005 29 596.

14.7 RADBOD

Approach: Follow the E39 from Ørsta or Volda and turn off in the direction of Ulsteinvik at the large roundabout, drive through two land tunnels on the RV653, but turn off towards Sørheim before entering the subsea tunnel. Park by a gravel-filled breakwater at Selbervik. The wreck of the DS Radbod lies just 200 metres from the shore, but we recommend that you dive from a boat. If you have no boat available, you can swim 200 metres out to the buoy and follow the rope down to the bow at a depth of 25 metres.

The wreck: The DS Radbod was sunk by British Beaufighter planes on 5th December 1944, after the convoy of which Radbod was a part was discovered in the Ørstafjord. British warplanes came swooping in over the Sunnmøre mountains and dived towards the vessels on the fjord. Radbod suffered a number of direct hits in the machine room just below the water-line from rockets and cannons. Less than two hours after the alarm was sounded, Radbod came to rest on the bottom of the Ørstafjord. All the crew were rescued and taken onboard one of the other ships in the convoy.

Description: The wreck of the 115-metre long vessel is relatively intact and lies in a stable position on a slope on the seabed. The enormous dimensions make the wreck a great subject for photography. The bow of Radbod is sharp and steep and worth a visit in its own right. Although the wreck lies in deep water, as a scuba diver you can enjoy a good dive down to 25-35 metres, and it is quite possible to look inside the wreck in the "shallow" section from 30-40 metres. But be careful – the wreck lies on a slope, and you can quickly end up diving too deep.

Depth: 25-80 metres.

Certification: CMAS***, PADI advanced or technical certification if you plan to dive deeper than 30-40 metres.

GPS position: 62°12' N 06°02'E

14.8 GRASØYANE

Approach: Here we recommend that you contact Herøy Scuba Diving Club for local guiding and hire of a boat.

Description: Grasøyane consists of several small islets and rocks. A colony of seals lives here, and if you are lucky, they will become inquisitive and come up pretty close. Remember that you are not allowed to anchor closer than 50 metres from land during the period 15th April – 15th August.

Depth: 1-10 metres.

Certification: Basic course CMAS, PADI or equivalent.

GPS position: N 62°25.52 E005°45.28'

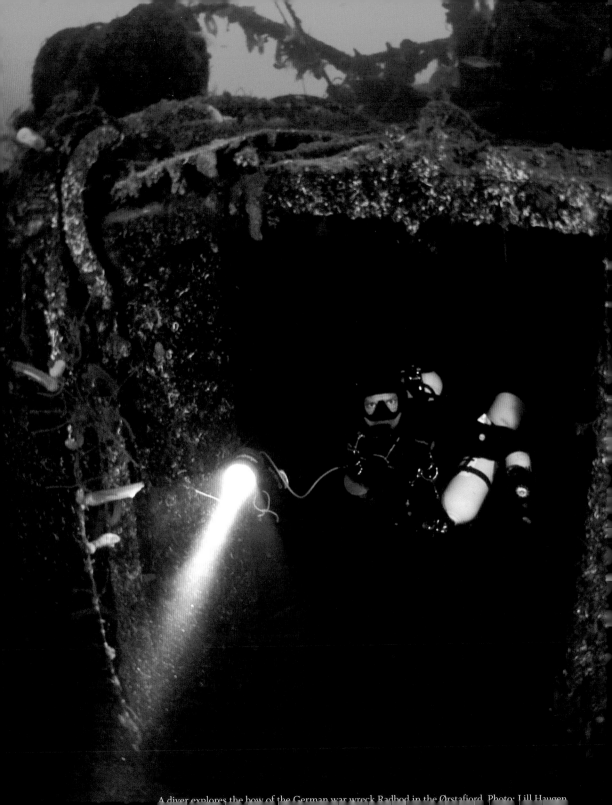

A diver explores the bow of the German war wreck Radbod in the Ørstafjord. Photo: Lill Haugen

A mysterious creature deep below the surface – the beautiful plankton "Sea angel" (Clione limacina). Photo: Lill Hauger

14.9 LYGNSTØYLVATNET

Approach: Drive from Ørsta to Sæbø on the RV655. Take the ferry Sæbø-Lekneset. Drive on past Hotel Union at Øye and continue up the valley. After a few kilometres you will come to a lake on your left-hand side. Park by the information board.

Description: Norangsdalen is one of the narrowest and most spectacular valleys in Norway. It is surrounded by wild and beautiful scenery, and you can see the remains of the old summer farm that still lies on the valley bottom beneath the water. Lygnstøylvatnet was formed in 1908 when a huge rock-slide blocked the river that runs through the valley. The entire seter was swallowed up by the water: the fences, fishing spots by the river, the road itself and all the farm buildings, along with the thick forest of alder with its birds' nests, eggs and young birds. It is a very special experience to swim through the woods at a depth of 10 metres, or along the road with the remains of the fences and guard stones that are still standing there below the water, as if nothing had happened.

Depth: Below 10 metres there is nothing more to see.

Certification: Basic course/free diver.

Lakebed: Mud and sludge, green algae, remains of trees and old buildings.

A really unique diving experience is yours to be had at the submerged remains of the farm in Lygnstøylvatnet. Photo: Lill Haugen

173

15 LONGBOARDING

Downhill skateboarding is at it´s best in Sunnmøre. In this chapter we will describe four excellent down-hill courses in the region. We start in the inland part of the area – close to Trollvegen in Romsdalen – and end up far west on the coast at West Cape. Along the route there will be many other downhill co-urses that you can discover for yourself. Generally speaking Sunnmøre is extremely well suited to long-boarding with all its many large and small mountain passes and steep hills. Here you can travel around between tourist attractions and beauty spots and discover new and untested downhill courses. The standard of the roads and the quality of the tarmac surfaces varies a great deal, and it is worth making a note of how this is linked to the classification of roads as local council roads, county council roads (FV), national roads (RV) or international E-roads. The local authority roads often have the poorest surface, but also least traffic. The European roads usually enjoy the best standard, but also the highest volume of traffic. Longboarding is not at all common on the roads of Sunnmøre. Many drivers can be scared stiff if a longboarder hurtles past their car on a steep and narrow road. So show respect for other road users.

High-speed boarding on the upper section of Trollstigen. Kongen in the background. Photo: Eirik Vaage

15.1   TROLLSTIGEN (750 m)

Welcome to the time-honoured Trollstigen Mountain Road. This main road has been given the status of national tourist highway, and not without reason. Trollstigen was completed in 1936 – after a construction period lasting all of eight years. The road is a really impressive sight from the viewing platform at Stigøra and the line of the road will set your pulse racing. It has only eleven hairpin bends, but on the other hand they wind their way up a steep valley surrounded by monumental mountains on both sides. Trollstigen is the third most visited tourist destination in Norway, and the road itself is the main attraction.

Length:	6 km.
Gradient:	8-10 degrees.
Hazards:	Large volume of traffic and narrow road. At times of high water flow, the road surface is often wet for 30 metres on both sides of the bridge where the road crosses the waterfall at Stigefoss bru.
Approach:	From Oslo/Trondheim you take the E6 towards Dombås. Turn off onto the E136 towards Åndalsnes, but take the RV63 15 km before Åndalsnes. Follow the RV63 through Isterdalen to Trollstigen. From Ørsta you take the E39 towards Molde. Turn off onto the E136 just before Vestnes, in the direction of Åndalsnes. Drive 15 km past Åndalsnes and take the RV63 to Trollstigen.
Description:	The downhill course starts at the new tourist centre at the top of Trollstigen. The road is old and the upper section is both narrow and airy. The first three hairpin bends have a diameter of 10 metres and are on the edge of a precipice. After the third hairpin you pass the 180 metre high waterfall Stigefossen, which at times with a high volume of water makes the road surface wet. It is worth noticing that the road enters the bridge on a 25-degree bend! Below the bridge the width of the road has mostly been upgraded. The standard of the lower section of Trollstigen is good. After nine bends and about 4.5 km downhill you come to a long stretch with just a gentle slope. Here Trollstigfoten is situated – a viewing platform for tourists. On down the Isterdalen valley you can cruise down 8 km of gentle gradient, ending up at the entrance to Romsdalen – about 20 km from Trollveggen. Trollstigen has a very high volume of traffic from its opening in May until it closes for the winter in October, the majority of which is made up of tourists. This means that much of the traffic consists of mobile homes, which take up a lot of space on the road. These vehicles often drive very slowly down Trollstigen. Especially on the upper section of Trollstigen, overtaking is a challenge because the road is very narrow.

15.2 ØRNEVEGEN (600 moh.)

«The Eagles Road» consists of eleven hairpin bends that stretch from the fjord at Grande and up to the mountain pass at Korsmyra. Ørnevegen is the only way to get to Geiranger by road during the winter.

Length: 6 km.
Gradient: 8-10 degrees.
Hazards: Large volume of tourist traffic.
Approach: From Oslo/Trondheim you take the E6 to Otta. Here you turn off onto the RV15 passing Lom on the way towards Stryn. Drive a few kilometres past the mountain hotel at Grotli on Strynefjell and then turn right onto the RV63 towards Geiranger. Follow the road through the centre of Geiranger and out along the fjord for 1 km and then climb up to the top of the Ørnevegen hairpins. From Ørsta you take the RV655 to Sæbø. Take the ferry from Sæbø – Lekneset and continue through the Norangsdal until you reach the RV60, where you turn left and head down to Hellesylt. Take the ferry up the Geirangerfjord, and turn left on disembarking. Drive out along the fjord for 1 km and then climb to the top of the Ørnesvegen hairpins.
Description: The downhill course starts at the Korsmyra picnic area. To begin with there is a gentle gradient down towards the Ørnevegen hairpins, but 500 metres before the first bend it becomes much steeper and you can cruise at 60 km pr hour. In general Ørnevegen is a steep road, but you have fairly good visibility ahead of you. It is also possible to glance over the safety barrier to check whether there is traffic approaching round the next hairpin. After eleven hairpin bends and about 6 km downhill, you end up beside the Geiranger-fjord, about 1 km from the centre of Geiranger.

Not what tourists on the viewing platform above Ørnesvingane expected to see. Photo: Eirik Vaage

15.3   DALSNIBBEVEGEN (1472 m)

This is one of Norway's best downhill courses. The road climbs to a height of 1472 metres, but unfortunately the first 400 metres down from the summit are a gravel road. From the Djupvatnet lake there is tarmac all the way down to the ferry quay in the centre of Geiranger. It is a really special experience to run from a mountain peak above the tree limit right down to the shore of the fjord, especially when it means rounding over thirty bends in the space of 17 km downhill. The changes in the landscape from 1050 metres above sea level down to just one metre above the fjord are unique, and it is not without reason that Geiranger is on UNESCO's World Heritage list. We recommend a refreshing dip in the Geirangerfjord after the run.

Length: 17 km.
Gradient: 8-10 degrees.
Hazards: Cattle grids and often a lot of mobile homes on the road.
Approach: From Oslo/Trondheim you take the E6 to Otta. Here you turn off onto the RV15 passing Lom on the way towards Stryn. Drive a few kilometres past the mountain hotel at Grotli on Strynefjell and then turn right onto the RV63 towards Geiranger. Stop by the lake at Djupvatnet and rig your equipment. From Ørsta you take the RV655 to Sæbø. Take the ferry from Sæbø – Lekneset and continue through the Norangdal until you reach the RV60, where you turn left and head down to Hellesylt. Take the ferry up the Geirangerfjord, and after disembarking in Geiranger drive up the RV63 to the lake at Djupvatnet.
Description: The tarmaced stretch of Dalsnibbevegen starts at the lake and descends gently through an open treeless landscape with long, sweeping bends. After 4 km the road becomes steeper and a magnificent stretch including twelve hairpin bends takes you down to 500m. Here the road levels out again, and you come to a cattle grid that is signposted. 1 km after the cattle grid the road rounds the bend by the Utsikten Hotel, which stands on the edge of a vantage point. Below the hotel the road becomes steeper, and yet another great stretch with six hairpin bends takes you down to the centre of Geiranger. On the final section of the road the speed will be very high, and you will finish the run with a top speed of 60-70 km per hour along the Geirangerfjord.

Longboarders on their way down Dalsnibbevegen. The Geirangerfjord in the background. Photo: Eirik Vaage

15.4   STRYNEFJELLSVEGEN (1000 m)

Strynefjellsvegen was opened in 1894 and at the time was the main overland link between the northwest region of Southern Norway and the eastern region. In 1977 a new road was built including three tunnels between Grotli and Ospeli bru. Thus the original road became known as Gamle Strynefjellsvegen, which has now been awarded status as a national tourist highway, and the stretch from Grotli to the summer skiing area is still a gravel road. But this is not a problem for anyone wishing to downhill, since the old road has been tarmaced from the ski centre area to Ospeli bru, where the old road meets the new (RV15) just below the final tunnel and above the hairpin bends.

Length: Alternative 1: 7 km. Alternative 2: 8 km.
Gradient: Alternative 1: 8-10 degrees. Alternative 2: 7-8 degrees.
Hazards:
Alternative 1: Poor quality tarmac in places and narrow road.
Alternative 2: Heavy traffic, a bridge on a hairpin bend and cattle grid immediately after bend 9.
Approach: From Oslo/Trondheim you take the E6 to Otta. Here you turn off onto the RV15 passing Lom on the way towards Stryn. Drive as far as Grotli Hotel high on the mountain pass. You can either turn left onto the old road Gamle Strynefjellsvegen (RV258) when this is open or continue until you leave the third tunnel immediately before the descent from the mountains begins and turn left up Gamle Strynefjellsvegen in the direction of Grotli. Stop at the summer skiing centre. From Volda you follow the E39 (from September 2012) in the direction of Stryn / Oslo. About 6.5 km after the centre of Hornindal you turn left onto the RV15 and continue on that road through the centre of Stryn. After climbing the hairpins, turn right immediately before the first tunnel onto Gamle Strynefjellsvegen in the direction of Grotli. Continue until you reach the summer ski centre. If you need overnight accommodation, we recommend the legendary Folven camping at the foot of the mountains on the Stryn side.
Description: There are two alternative stretches to descend:
Alternative 1: Gamle Strynefjellsvegen. This starts at the Stryn Summer Ski Centre and goes down the old mountain road. This is usually opened for traffic after the winter in late May/early June, but this will vary from year to year. If you run this downhill course immediately after the opening, you will have 5 meter high walls of snow that form a corridor along the road. The road is about 7 km long and there is little traffic, but on the other hand the road is narrow and the tarmac of poor quality. The first 4 km have a gradient of 7-8 degrees and eight bends. The road passes through an open treeless landscape. As you pass Videseter Hotel the road becomes steeper, and you can enjoy six beautiful hairpin bends that are fairly demanding technically speaking. Be aware of low crash barriers and poor quality road surface.

Alternative 2: Strynefjellsvingane. These hairpin bends begin where alternative 1 ends, at the Ospeli tunnel, which is known as «The Gateway to Western Norway». This is the RV15, which is one of the mountain passes in Norway that has the densest volume of traffic. For this reason the road is of a far better standard than the other roads described in this chapter,

Cruising down the hairpins on Strynefjellsvegen. Photo: Eirik Vaage

which have far less traffic. Strynefjellsvingane from the Ospeli tunnel is almost like a motorway by comparison with a steady gradient of 7-8 degrees. Here you can maximise your speed and slide round the bends. There is heavy traffic, but the wide road offers reasonably safe driving conditions. On the seventh bend after the tunnel you cross a bridge. Below the bridge the road flattens out somewhat, before you come to an s-bend. Immediately after the bend there is a cattle grid. On the remaining stretch down to Folven campsite you can cruise comfortably without encountering any bends.

Narrow twists and turns on the way down to Hoddevika. Photo: Eirik Vaage

Rounding a hairpin bend on the Hoddeviksvingane. Photo: Eirik Vaage

15.5 HODDEVIKSSVINGANE (300 moh.)

West Cape (Stadtlandet) has a number of downhill courses, but the most characteristic is Hoddevik-svingane. Hairpin bends with a view of the Atlantic Ocean are indeed a rarity, and Hoddevikdalen is a beautiful lush green valley. Even though the course is modest by comparison to the other courses in this chapter, you will be able to downhill all the way to the westernmost metre of tarmac in Norway.

Length:	4-5 km.
Gradient:	7-8 degrees.
Hazards:	Narrow road and low barrier. Cattle grid 100 metres after bend 6.
Approach:	Take the ferry from the centre of Volda to Lauvstad and follow the RV652 to Syvde and Eidså. Then turn left onto the RV61 to Åheim. Continue along the RV620 all the way to Leikanger. Turn left in Leikanger, and then sharp left again towards Hoddevika. Stop at the highest point between Drage and Hoddevika and rig your equipment.
Description:	The downhill course starts at the highest point between Drage and Hoddevika. The first kilometer the gradient is fairly gentle, but your speed is high in the thick pine forest before you come to the bends. The road is narrow and the tarmac is of poor quality. But the unique scenery and the view towards the coast at Hoddevikstranda still make it worth driving this short downhill course. There are seven bends in all, and six of them are hair-pin bends with low safety barriers.

16 WINDSURFING AND KITESURFING

Of the above activities it is windsurfing that has the longest traditions in Sunnmøre. But the long coastline also provides excellent conditions for kitesurfing. Certain places are well-established and widely known, while others are well-kept secrets. There is every opportunity of finding one's own little eldorado here. Sunnmøre also offers good opportunities for kiting on snow. There is already some kiting activity on Ørskogfjellet, in the Tafjordfjella and at most of the ski resorts. But you also have the chance of discovering your own kiteskiing spot in the Sunnmøre Alps.

Windsurfing in strong winds and high seas on the coast. Photo: Annemor Larsen

16.1 OLMANESET
VIGRA

Approach: Drive over the bridge between Valderøya and Vigra in the direction of the airport. Leave the main road immediately after the golf course on Vigra, at the signpost "Flyplass" (airport). Turn right onto a private road. Right after the large pine hedge belonging to the first house, take a sharp right turn onto a farm track, then to the left by the sea, where you park.

Wind: Olmaneset is the spot where the north-easterly wind is strongest. The wind speed here is normally 1-2 m/sec stronger here than at Roaldsanden.

Hazards: When the wind gets up, you need to be careful here. If it is 10 m/sec at Roaldsanden, it can easily be 15-16 m/sec at Olmaneset. Don't lose your rig here, because then you'll be in for a long walk back to the car. This spot is not for beginners, who can easily end up in the rocks on the beach a couple of hundred metres further down the coast.

16.2 ROALDSANDEN
VIGRA

Approach: Drive over the bridge between Valderøya and Vigra, drive past the airport and on to Roald. Park by the school up on the road. During the summer holidays and after school hours you can use the school car park and walk across the school playground.

Wind: Functional in a north-easterly, but the spot is best in an east/north-easterly, which provides a stable onshore wind. This is the best place for beginners, since it is shallow so far out. You can stand up to your waist in water a long way out and surf in towards the shore on the onshore wind.

Hazards: A small sandbank causes the formation of a tiny lagoon with calm water 2-3 hours before and after low water. It is very shallow here. At this time you need to be in full control of what you are doing, because the depth of water is just a few centimetres here. There are also few rocks in the area, but these are easy to see.

16.3 BLIMSANDEN
VIGRA

Approach: Drive over the bridge between Valderøya and Vigra. Turn left towards Synes immediately after the bridge. Turn right 300 metres after you have passed the end of the airport runway, immediately after a small video kiosk. Keep straight ahead as far as you can go, and turn left at the end of the road, before turning right when you see the signpost "Blimsanden".

Wind: This location is best in northerly, north-westerly and westerly winds. Then the wind is onshore and crosses onshore. The sandy beach is large with plenty of room to rig and to bathe. The spot is also suitable for beginners.

Hazards: None in particular.

VIGRA/GISKE/GODØYA

Approach: Take the first exit at the large roundabout just before the centre of Ålesund and drive down into the subsea tunnel on the RV658 in the direction of Vigra/Giske/Godøya. After you emerge from the second tunnel, you are on the island of Valderøya. Now you can either turn left towards the neighbouring island of Giske and on to the island of Godøya, or keep straight ahead to the island of Vigra.

Flying high off the island of Godøya. Photo: Nikolai Melseth Flaaen

16.4 GISKEBRUA
GISKE

Approach: Turn left at the first junction as soon as you emerge from the second subsea tunnel from Ålesund, and you will immediately find Giskebrua (the large bridge). There are fine sandy beaches ideal for rigging, camping and barbecuing on both sides of the bridge.

Wind: The north-easterly wind here is normally not as strong as at Olmaneset.

Hazards: This spot is not recommended for beginners in a north-easterly (onshore) wind. There is a danger of ending up too close to the bridge foundations and road causeway. On the leeside the water is calm but the north-easterly is extremely variable. The power lines on the furthest point of the headline also represent a very real danger. Near the bridge the wind and the currents often go in opposite directions.

16.5 ALNES
GODØYA

Approach: Turn left at the first junction as soon as you emerge from the second subsea tunnel from Ålesund, drive over Giskebrua (the bridge) and take the RV658 to Alnes on the island of Godøya. Park by the lighthouse.

Wind: The venue offers good conditions in all westerly wind directions. If you look at the wave height predictions for West Cape (Stadhavet) you can as a rule subtract about two metres with regard to the wave height around Alnes.

Hazards: Large waves, a short stretch of shoreline and a lot of rocks. The spot is totally unsuitable for beginners, but for more experienced windsurfers Alnes at times offers plenty of good surfing.

16.6 KVALNESET
GISKE

Approach: Drive as far as you can on Giske. Here you must park by the road barrier and walk the gravel road 300 metres to the beach.

Wind: The venue offers good conditions in all wind directions apart from southerly and south-westerly, when the wind is offshore and variable.

Hazards: There are some rocks in the area, but the water is usually clear, which means it is easy to catch sight of the rocks, which for the most part lie close to land.

Classic windsurfing off the coast of Godøya. Alnes lighthouse in the background. Photo: Nikolai Melseth Flaaen

16.7 FLØ
ULSTEINVIK

Approach: Follow the E39 from Ørsta or Volda and take the road to Ulsteinvik at the large roundabout, drive through two road tunnels and the deep subsea tunnel. Follow the RV653 to
Ulsteinvik and follow the signposts to Flø. From Ålesund you can take the E136, E39 and
RV61 to the ferry Sulesund – Hareid. Stay on the RV61 to Ulsteinvik and then follow the
signposts to Flø. Stop at Flø Feriesenter.

Wind: Excellent in northerly, north-westerly and to some extent in north-easterly winds. Flø can
offer wonderful conditions with cross-shore winds and waves coming straight at you. In a
north-easterly the waves at Flø are smaller, but the wind is often much stronger from this
direction.

Hazards: There can be some turbulence close to land.

16.8 VOLDSFJORDEN
VOLDA

Approach: Start from the ferry quay in the centre of Volda or from the special windsurfers' boathouse on the shore a few hundred metres further west down the fjord.

Wind: This spot has more wind than most places along the coast, but only when the wind is
from the south or the north. In the spring there can a lot of northerly winds, and in fine
weather the wind strength will normally be 3-4 m/sec stronger than out on the coast. The
wind force is very stable, but it can often be difficult to get out from the shore or to come
ashore. In the summer there is often a good sunwise breeze in the afternoon. The fjord is
more suitable for experienced windsurfers.

Hazards: Keep a sharp lookout for the ferry traffic!

Kiting on the Voldsfjord. Photo: Eirik Vaage

17   SURFING

Stadlandet has established itself as one of Norway's best and most visited surfing locations, and especially in Hoddevika and Ervika you will find very popular spots. Stadlandet is not the easiest place in the world to get to, but once you are there, you will in return find good overnight accommodation right beside the surfing beaches. In Hoddevika alone there are four hostels with a total of 75 beds.

It was surfing enthusiasts from Volda who from the start in 1997 established what has gradually become a very distinct surfing culture in Hoddevika. Soon after the year 2000 the first surfing motel was opened, and in the following years two other establishments were opened. At this time the average age of the local population was 65, but surfers who moved there and visiting surfers have reversed the negative demographic trend in the village and have helped to give it a completely new atmosphere and energy. In the surfing season it is not uncommon to find 50 to 100 youths in this tiny village.

A magic moment courtesy of a big one at Ervika. Photo: Thomas Bickhardt

17.1   HODDEVIKA

Approach: Take the ferry from the centre of Volda to Lauvstad, and follow the RV652 to Syvde and Eidså. There turn left along the RV61 to Åheim. Then follow the RV620 all the way to Leikanger. Turn left in Leikanger and then turn sharp left again onto the RV632 to Hoddevika.

Conditions: The valley has a length of two kilometres and at the beach is about 800 metres across. A shiny white sandy beach stretches from one side of the valley to the other, and 400 metre-high mountains surround the valley and continue right out towards the sea. Hoddevikstranda has for the most part a sandy bottom, but the northern end of the beach has a stony bottom. Beachbreaks break along the whole of the huge beach, and as a rule there is a choice of many waves to surf on. The conditions on the seabed vary a great deal, but we will roughly divide Hoddevikstranda into three zones: Peach, Mediterranean and Sørenden (the south end).

Peach: Here you will find a righthander that can run all the way from the harbour wall and in to the beach. The best conditions are at high water and low water. It is a medium quick wave that rarely has a tube. Under optimum conditions you can surf about 200 metres.

Mediterranean: Here you find an A-frame wave that starts from the centre of the beach and runs about 100 metres in both directions. The surf is very dependent on the seabed conditions. There are often quicker and larger waves here than at Peach. There may be a tube at high water and with an offshore wind.

Sørenden (aka 'dead man beach'):   Here you find a lefthander which with good seabed conditions and offshore wind can produce good, long, steep waves. Generally the seabed consists of sand with some boulders on the north and south sides of the bay.

Wind: NE to SW gives offshore. W to N gives onshore.

Advice: Paddle out from the harbour wall if the waves are overhead.

Hazards: When there are large waves, it can be dangerous to stand on the harbour wall. Many surfers have been injured when large waves have washed them off the harbour wall. If you get swept out into the water and do not have a surfboard to support you, the current will quickly take hold of you. Sørenden has a strong current which when the sea is running high can easily sweep a man off his feet. The current can transport you a good way out into the bay. Paddle towards the middle of the bay if you experience strong currents.

Every surfer's dream in Hoddevika. Photo: Eirik Vaage

17.2 ERVIKA

Approach: Take the ferry from the centre of Volda to Lauvstad, and follow the RV652 to Syvde and Eidså. There turn left along the RV61 to Åheim. Then follow the RV620 all the way to Leikanger. Turn left in Leikanger and then sharp right again onto the RV633 in the direction of Ervika. Follow the RV45 the final stretch to Ervika.

Conditions: In Ervika you will find the westernmost of all the surfing spots at Stadlandet. Ervikdalen is rich in cultural heritage with clear traces of settlements as far back as the Viking Age. The valley is about 8 km long and surrounded by mountains, but these are lower than those surrounding Hoddevika. The densest settlement is to be found at the far end of the valley, right on the beach at Ervikstranda. The very special graveyard in Ervika lies up on a mound with a view across the beach and is a moving reminder of the fact that the sea both gives and takes. Ervikstranda has for the most part a sandy bottom, but the northern

The ocean gives and the ocean takes. Photo: Eirik Vaage

end, from the graveyard north, has rocks along the shore. Waves break along the entire length of the 400 metre beach and as a rule you have many different spots to surf on. The seabed conditions vary a good deal. It is difficult to define distinct lines in Ervika.

In general the waves at Ervika are about one meter higher than those in Hoddevika, and Ervika is somewhat more exposed to wind, especially side winds. On days when the wind and surf is really running high, Ervikstranda can be quite a challenge even for experienced surfers. Days with offshore winds can give large waves and short tubes and technically demanding surf. The seabed consists of sand with some boulders on the north end.

Wind: NE to SW gives offshore. W to N gives onshore.

Advice: Paddle out from the cliffs on the north side of the bay. You will often find a good right hand wave when you are in line with the graveyard.

Hazards: There is an ancient shipwreck roughly in the centre of the beach (150 metres south of the graveyard).

17.3   ÅRVIKA

Approach: Take the ferry from the centre of Volda to Lauvstad, and follow the RV652 to Syvde and Eidså. There turn left along the RV61 to Åheim. Then follow the RV620 all the way to Leikanger. Turn left in Leikanger and then sharp right again onto the RV633 in the direction of Ervika. Follow the RV45 the final stretch to Årvika.

Conditions: Årvika is a small bay north of Ervika, with a tiny hamlet that nestles on the edge of this small beach. The bay faces due northwest. The south end of the bay stretches far out to sea and has a huge perpendicular rock face that provides shelter from the westerly wind. Because the south end of the bay is so long, there are few waves on the beach. The point break 250 metres south of the beach is, however, an interesting place. The spot is suitable only for experienced surfers since it only works on headhigh +. The point can tolerate high seas. The waves are medium-calm with few tubes. When conditions are too overwhelming in Ervika, Årvika is often fine, and even with double headhigh the line is good for experienced surfers. The seabed consists of boulders and sand.

Wind: SE to SW gives offshore. NW to N gives onshore. Årvika is often in lee of the westerly wind.

Advice: Årvika is not a place for beginners, but at the same time Årvika is often safer than Ervika on a big day, not because the waves are smaller, but because there is pointbreak.

Hazards: Årvika-waves break along the shore – about 50 metres from cliffs and huge boulders.

Preparing for the really big one in Eltvika. Photo: Eirik Vaage

17.4   ELTVIKA

Approach: Take the ferry from the centre of Volda to Lauvstad, and follow the RV652 to Syvde and Eidså. There turn left along the RV61 to Åheim. Then follow the RV620 all the way to Leikanger. Continue straight ahead along the north-east side of Stadlandet, past Borgundvåg, and right to the end of the road.

Conditions: The point breaker is a lefthander that runs about 50 metres on a good day. The point must have a minimum of 4 metres of sea from NW to NE in order to function. The point lies close to cliffs. The wave starts in a tube-section on big days and is a medium-quick wave. The seabed consists of boulders.

Wind: W to SE gives offshore. NW to E gives onshore.

Advice: Eltvika is only suitable for experienced surfers, with a technically demanding wave that breaks right below cliffs. The advantage is that the current drags you away from the point, which means you get good help from the current if you wipeout and come on the inside.

Hazards: The wave is powerful and breaks right below cliffs. The current is strong, and it can be difficult to get back ashore.

17.5   DRAGE

Approach: Take the ferry from the centre of Volda to Lauvstad, and follow the RV652 to Syvde and Eidså. There turn left along the RV61 to Åheim. Then follow the RV620 all the way to Leikanger. Turn left in Leikanger and then sharp left again onto the RV632 in the direction of Hoddevika, but turn left onto the RV43 to Drage.

Conditions: Drage lies on the south of Stadlandet and is actually a calm bay that is relatively well protected from the storms that rage from the southwest and northwest. It was at Drage that the Vikings came ashore with their longboats and dragged them over the ridge to Leikanger when the weather was bad. Drage takes in waves from the west. In high seas SW and NW can also work. If the waves in Hoddevika are too big, it is possible that you can surf at Drage. Boulders dominate the beach. There are relatively short lines along the whole of the beach.

Wind: N to E gives offshore. SE to NW gives onshore.

Advice: If the forecast is high seas from W, it can be worth checking to see if conditions are better at Drage.

Hazards: None in particular.

It's not every day the skiing is this good on Stad. Hoddevika in the background. Photo: Eirik Vaage

18 TRAVEL AND ACCOMMODATION
18.1 TRAVEL

AIR

The regional airport at Ålesund Vigra has direct connections (www.sas.no or www.norwegian.no) to the Norwegian cities of Oslo, Bergen, Stavanger, Trondheim and Haugesund. In addition there are several international routes with direct flights, among others from London, Copenhagen, Alicante and Riga. You can fly to Ørsta-Volda airport Hovden (www.wideroe.no) from Oslo and Bergen. Bus transport is provided from both airports and into the town centres. However, it is not easy to travel by bus in Sunnmøre, and if you are planning a trip in the great outdoors, it is virtually impossible to take a bus. Therefore it is better to rent a car (www.hertz.no or www.avis.no) at the airport.

TRAIN

From Oslo and Trondheim Central Stations there are daily trains to Åndalsnes, which lies about 120 km from Ålesund. From Åndalsnes there are buses five times a day to and from Ålesund. The train journey through the Romsdal valley gives you a chance to see Trollveggen. For further information on timetables and prices see www.nsb.no.

BUS

There are express coach services all across the region with good connections to Oslo, Bergen and Trondheim. Use Norway bussekspress (www.nor-way.no), which is Norway's largest express coach company. Within the region you can use TIMEekspressen (www.timeekspressen.no) , which departs hourly from Volda/Ørsta, via Ålesund to Molde and Kristiansund and return. All types of local bus routes can be found at the bus and ferry company Fjord1 (www.fjord1.no). For information on timetables and prices of ferries and buses in Sunnmøre, you can also telephone 177, 175 and from abroad +47 71 58 78 00.

CAR

Oslo-Ålesund: Take the E6 to Dombås. Then take the E136 via Åndalsnes to Ålesund. On your way down the Romsdal valley you will drive past Trollveggen. This is a really spectacular drive!
Oslo-Volda/Ørsta: Take the E6 to Otta. Then turn left onto the RV15 via Stryn towards Nordfjordeid, before joining the E39 to Volda and Ørsta at Grodås. In the summer you can also leave the RV15 soon after Grotli on Strynefjellet and take the RV63 to Geiranger. Take the ferry from Geiranger to Hellesylt, and follow the RV655 via the ferry Lekneset-Sæbø and on to Ørsta. This is a fascinating drive that you will not forget in a hurry!
Bergen-Volda/Ørsta/Ålesund: Follow the E39 all the way north.
Trondheim-Ålesund/Ørsta/Volda: Follow the E39 all the way south.

DISTANCES

Ålesund - Oslo 520 km (8 hours)
Ålesund - Bergen 370 km (6 hours 30 minutes)
Ålesund - Trondheim 285 km (4 hours and 30 minutes)

PLANNING YOUR JOURNEY

www.google.com, www.visveg.no, www.gulesider.no, www.177mr.no

ROAD CLASSIFICATION SYSTEM IN NORWAY

The most important Norwegian roads are classified in a three-tier system. The major roads belong to the European (E) trunk road system. The other two tiers consist of national (RV) and county (FV) road networks. In other words, in this book you will find references such as the E39, the RV655 and the FV137 respectively.

FERRIES

If you see Sunnmøre from the air, you will be struck by a pattern of islands and peninsulas surrounded by fjords and fjord arms. This means that many stretches include ferry crossings, although some of these have been replaced by subsea tunnels in recent years. It is therefore extremely important to keep yourself updated about the ferry timetables when you are planning any journey in this region. On most of the ferries you can purchase refreshments. The largest ferry company in Sunnmøre is Fjord 1 (www.fjord1.no) but also Tide (www.tide.no) now operates many of the ferry connections.

The ferry approaching land at Sæbø. Slogen in the background. Photo: Eirik Vaage

18.2   ACCOMMODATION

Public right of access is an integral part of Norway's cultural heritage. In open country you can move freely everywhere either on foot or on skis and stop to take a break wherever you like. Sleeping under open skies or in a tent is permitted in outlying land, but no closer than 150 metres from an inhabited dwelling, house or cabin. If you intend to stay longer than two days at the same spot, the landowner must give you permission. Even so, you can camp in a tent for as long as you like if you do so far from any house or in the high mountains. The public right of access also means that you may freely pick any type of berry, mushroom and plant that is not protected on outlying land by a conservation order. This ancient right assumes that you will take care of and show respect for our natural environment. Whatever you bring with you on your trips into natural surroundings, must be taken back, and the only traces of your activity that you are allowed to leave behind are your footprints. For further details about the public right of access, see the website: www.miljostatus.no.

SETER

In Scandinavia, transhumance – the seasonal movement of people and their livestock to a summer pasture in the mountains to graze – has long traditions and is in fact still practised. In Norwegian the word seter is used to describe this place, a word that comes from the Old Norse sætr, referring to a custom that is probably as old as the origins of the word itself. Livestock were typically tended by girls and younger women who milked and made cheese. Often a seter consisted of no more than a tiny wooden hut for the milkmaids to live in, while others had two or three rooms and perhaps even a separate barn for the animals. Many of these old seters have been left to deteriorate at the mercy of the elements, so that just the stone foundations remain today, but they may also have been turned into cabins and summer homes for families and tourists. The term seter, used to describe this summer farm or mountain pasture, is to be found frequently as part of many of the local place names or locations referred to in this guide, and has therefore been used in the text in a number of contexts.

MEMBERSHIP IN ORGANISATIONS

THE NORWEGIAN TREKKING ASSOCIATION (DNT)

Members of The Norwegian Trekking Association are offered large discounts on overnight accommodation and your own door key to any one of the association's 460 cabins all over Norway. Some of the lodges are staffed, but most of them are self-catering cabins with a store of food that may be purchased. If you are not a member, you may borrow a standard DNT cabin key from any DNT office against a deposit. Note that it is impossible to know how many people are staying at any one cabin until you actually arrive there. The unwritten rule, however, is that "where there is room in the heart, there is always room in the house". So someone will usually give you a mattress on the floor even if the cabin is full when you get there.

Prices: Members/Non-members
Accommodation (inc. breakfast at staffed lodges) NOK 280 / 430. Discounts for youth, children and families.

STAFFED LODGES
Season for staffed lodges
Reindalseter (95 beds) 27.06. – 30.08.
Kaldhusseter (43 beds) 04.06. – 16.08., both in the Tafjordfjella in Inner Sunnmøre.

SELF-CATERING CABINS
KYSTEN, OUTER SUNNMØRE: Runde lighthouse (17 beds).

SUNNMØRSALPANE, MID-SUNNMØRE: Standalhytta (10 beds), Patchellhytta (50 beds), Velleseter-hytta (9 beds) and Tyssenaustet (6 beds).

TAFJORDFJELLA, INNER SUNNMØRE: Danskehytta (26 beds), Fieldfarehytta (4 beds), Fokhaugstova (9 beds), Pyttbua (51 beds), Tjønnabu (9 beds), Tøssebrobu (18 beds), Vakkerstøylen (28 beds) and Velt-dalshytta (50 beds).

For more information, see www.turistforeningen.no and www.aast.no

HOSTELLING INTERNATIONAL NORWAY
Members of Hostelling International Norway are entitled to a 15% discount on the total price of accom-modation at Norwegian hostels. www.hihostels.no

ACCOMMODATION ALONG THE COAST, OUTER SUNNMØRE

HODDEVIKA
Here you will find one of Norway's best spots for surfing, with its own well-established surf camp. In addition to accommodation for 20 persons, you can hire surfing equipment and ocean-going kayaks, and you may sign up for a surfing course. There is also a small shop in Hoddevika.

Approach:	Take the ferry from the centre of Volda to Lauvstad, and follow the RV652 to Syvde and Eidså. There turn left along the RV61 to Åheim. Then follow the RV620 all the way to Leikanger. Turn left in Leikanger and then turn sharp left again onto the RV632 to Hoddevika.
Season:	Open all year round.
Prices 2010:	Student NOK 200 pr night. Others NOK 300 pr night. Bed linen NOK 50. Hire of surfing equipment (wetsuit and board) NOK 550 pr day. Surfing course including equipment NOK 950 pr day.
Address:	Torkild Strandvik, 6750 Stadlandet
Telephone:	+47 57 85 69 44
E-mail:	torkild@stadsurfing.com
Website:	www.stadsurfing.com

FISKÅ

HAKALLEGARDEN is a very friendly and attractive open farm with views across the Vanylvsfjord and out towards Stadlandet. Below the farm lies a beautiful sandy beach and a visitors' marina. In the converted cowshed there is a charming cosy cafe and shop. You can also stay the night in the lavvo in the farmyard at an affordable price.

Approach:	Take the ferry from the centre of Volda to Lauvstad, and follow the RV652 to Syvde and on to Fiskå. In Fiskå turn right towards Åram/Sandsøy. About 10 km after Fiskå you will find Hakallegarden on the left-hand side of the road.
Season:	June, July and August: Sunday-Monday 12-18. Rest of the year: Sundays 12-18.
Address:	Hakallestranda, 6149 Åram
Telephone:	+47 70 02 84 62 / 90 06 89 96
E-mail:	post@hakallegarden.no
Website:	www.hakallegarden.no

SANDSØYA

Skare Feriehus is perfectly situated with fishing, diving and other water activities in mind. There is a wonderful view out to sea across Stadhavet and Kvamsøya in the Vanylvsfjord. The area is peaceful and full of experiences of the great outdoors, especially on the water. There are also easy mountain hikes just a short distance from the cabins. Sandshamn marina with a shop, fishing equipment, petrol station and pub lies about 6 km from Skare. Accommodation prices include the use of a boat and boathouse. The cabins offer a high standard with a fully-equipped kitchen, bathroom, satellite-tv and a lovely outdoor area for barbecues. It is also possible to hire bicycles there.

Approach:	Follow the E39 from Ørsta or Volda and turn off in the direction of Ulsteinvik at the large roundabout, drive through two land tunnels and the long subsea tunnel. Follow the RV653 in the direction of Ulsteinvik, but turn off onto the RV61 and follow the road to Larsnes. Take the Larsnes-Vokså ferry and drive to Sandshamn. When you get there, turn left towards Sande. Follow the road along the south side of the island all the way to Skare.
Season:	Open all year round.
Prices 2010:	Ask about prices via e-mail or by phone.
Address:	Skare-Feriehus, Norunn & Peder Eltvik, 6089 Sandshamn
Telephone:	+47 70 02 90 18
E-mail:	skare@skare-feriehus.no
Website:	www.skare-feriehus.no

RUNDE

GOKSØYR CAMPING. Here you will be offered good help by local knowledgeable owners, who can also offer guiding in an area of stunning natural beauty which is also partly a nature reserve.

Approach:	Follow the E39 from Ørsta or Volda and turn off in the direction of Ulsteinvik at the large roundabout, drive through two land tunnels and the long subsea tunnel. Follow the RV653 in the direction of Ulsteinvik, but turn off onto the RV654 towards Fosnavåg a few kilometres after emerging from the final tunnel. Just before Fosnavåg, you turn right at the signpost to Runde. Drive along exciting roads and over spectacular bridges all the way out to the car park just before Goksøyra. The campsite is right beside the car park.

Season:	Open all year round.
Prices 2010:	Cabin for two: NOK 250 pr night. Tent: NOK 110 pr night.
Address:	Goksøyra, 6096 Runde
Telephone:	+47 70 08 59 05
Website:	www.goksoyr.no

RUNDE LIGHTHOUSE lies on the far north-west of the bird island of Runde in Herøy municipality. It is exciting to stay the night here facing the open sea and experience close at hand the enormous forces of nature. The newest keeper's dwelling has been converted into a self-catering cabin with 17 beds. The cabin is owned by The Norwegian Trekking Association (DNT), and you require a standard DNT-key to get in. It is possible to purchase dry foodstuffs from the self-service store in the cabin. The kitchen is well equipped with a fridge and kitchen utensils.

Approach:	Follow the same route as is described above for Goksøyr Camping. From the car park here it will take you about one and a half hours on a well marked footpath over the mountain and down to the lighthouse.
Season:	Open all year round.
Prices 2010:	Members: NOK 185 pr night. Non-members: NOK 285 pr night. Discounts for children, youths and families.
Telephone:	+47 70 06 11 17
Website:	www.aast.no

Runde lighthouse with nothing but the open sea beyond. Photo: Sindre Nakken

ULSTEINVIK

FLØ FERIESENTER lies right beside a wonderful sandy beach with great opportunities for bathing and surfing. It is also possible to take short mountain walks immediately behind the centre, and not least boulder on the huge rocks at the end of the road. The view out to sea across towards Stadhavet and the island of Runde is fantastic. The cabins, each of which sleeps 7, enjoy a modern standard with kitchen, bathroom and large patio for barbecues. In addition the centre has 30 sites for caravans and mobile homes with electricity supply, and also room for tents. For campers there is also a large communal kitchen available. Use of a boat is included in the cabin price, if you pay for the fuel.

Approach:	Follow the E39 from Ørsta or Volda and turn off in the direction of Ulsteinvik at the large roundabout, drive through two land tunnels and the long subsea tunnel. Follow the RV653 to Ulsteinvik, and then the signposts to Flø. From Ålesund you can follow the E136, E39 and the RV61 to the ferry from Sulesund-Hareid. Continue on the RV61 to Ulsteinvik, and then follow the signposts to Flø. Stop at Flø Feriesenter.
Season:	Open all year round.
Prices:	Peak season 10.06.-31.08. : NOK 900 pr night for cabin. Off-peak season: NOK 700 pr night for cabin.
Address:	Flø Feriesenter AS, 6065 Ulsteinvik
Telephone:	+47 70 01 50 80
E-mail:	flo.feriesenter@tussa.com
Website:	www.floe-feriesenter.no

ULSTEINVIK INTERNATIONAL HOSTEL was voted the best hostel in Norway in 2009. The building is a former SAS-hotel with very pleasant facilities in the centre of the town. There are good opportunities to train in a modern gymnasium right next door to the hostel. Short mountain hikes are also easy to do from right outside the hostel.

Approach:	Follow the E39 from Ørsta or Volda and turn off in the direction of Ulsteinvik at the large roundabout, drive through two land tunnels and the long subsea tunnel. Follow the RV653 all the way to the centre of Ulsteinvik. The hostel is on the left-hand side of the road. Breakfast is included in the price.
Season:	20.05. - 15.08.
Prices:	Single bed in dormitory: NOK 275 pr night. 4-bed room with private bathroom: NOK 850 pr night. Breakfast is included in the price. Towel: NOK 20. Bedlinen: NOK 60. Packed lunch: NOK 50.
Address:	Varleitvegen 5, 6065 Ulsteinvik
Telephone:	+47 70 00 9600
E-mail:	ulsteinvik@hihostels.no
Website:	www.hihostels.no/ulsteinvik

VIGRA

VESTAVIND BED AND BREAKFAST lies in a sheltered spot surrounded by the beauties of nature in every direction. The accommodation is ideal with bathing, fishing, diving, kiting and surfing in mind. The standard is high with a separate bathroom, communal kitchen and tv-room and a pleasant terrace for barbecues.

Approach:	Turn right at the roundabout just before the centre of Ålesund and drive down into the subsea tunnels on the RV658 in the direction of Vigra/Giske/Godøya. When you emerge from the second tunnel, you are on the island of Valderøya. Drive over the bridge onto the island of Vigra and on past the turning to the airport. When you come to a T-junction, turn left towards Synes. Drive 2 km along this road. Just before you come to the church, there is a sign saying "Vestavind Bed & Breakfast". Follow the road to the uppermost of the yellow and white houses.
Season:	Open all year round.
Prices:	NOK 600 pr person for B&B. NOK 820 for 2 persons in a double room.
Address:	Vestavind Gjestehus, 6040 Vigra
Telephone:	+47 70 18 27 33
E-mail:	vestavind@adsl.no
Website:	www.vestavindgjesthus.no

The footbridge across to Ulla lighthouse. Photo: Arnfinn Tønnesen

The Art Nouveau city of Ålesund seen from Fjellstua. Photo: Eirik Vaage

HARAMSØYA

ULLA FYR (the old lighthouse) is run by a group of volunteers keen to keep alive the old culture of the coast and the keeper's dwelling. Out here you can really enjoy the open sea, at the same time as there are good opportunities for bathing, fishing, diving and surfing. You can also go on bike rides of varying length and mountain walks starting from the lighthouse, which is subject to a protection order issued by the Directorate for Cultural Heritage in Norway. There are a total of 22 beds, divided among 6 rooms on the first floor of the main building. In the basement there are showers and vacuum toilets. The boathouse is included in the price, but can also be hired separately. There is seating for groups of up to 30 round the table in the dining room. The tenant is responsible for cleaning and normal check-out time is 12 noon. The lighthouse cafe is open during the summer. Ulla Fyr is a well-kept holiday house, with a well-equipped kitchen.

Approach:	Follow the E39 north from Ålesund in the direction of Brattvåg. Turn off left onto the RV661 at Digernes. Drive to Eidsvik, where you take a left turn onto the RV659. From Brattvåg you drive on towards Skjeltne, and take the ferry Skjeltne-Austnes. Head for the northern end of the island of Haramsøya and Ulla Fyr.
Season:	Open all year round.
Prices:	The whole premises NOK 2500 pr weekend + NOK 100 pr person for the use of a bed. Cost for each additional day: NOK 1250. Rent for half the building NOK 1250 pr weekend. Rent for the whole premises for one week NOK 4500.
Telephone:	+47 70 21 01 98
Website:	www.ullafyr.com
Telefon:	+47 70 21 01 98
Web:	www.ullafyr.com

ÅLESUND

ÅLESUND INTERNATIONAL HOSTEL is located right in the centre of the town. It has 72 beds divided among 17 rooms - singles, doubles and dormitory. The standard of the rooms, beds and service varies. Breakfast is included in the price during the summer season (01.05.- 30.09.).

Season:	Open all year round.
Prices:	NOK 225 pr night in a dormitory. Packed lunch NOK 55. Towel NOK 10.
Address:	Parkgata 14, 6003 Ålesund.
Telephone:	+47 70 11 58 30
E-mail:	aalesund@hihostels.no
Website:	www.hihostels.no

KOLÅS- OG RÅNAHALVØYA, MIDTRE SUNNMØRE

ØRSTA

STANDALHYTTA is owned by Ålesund Skiklubb (Aask) and offers good accommodation at a reasonable price. The lodge, which lies at the foot of Kolåstinden and which is one of the best summiting destinations in the Sunnmøre Alps, has about 40 beds available for large groups (minimum 15 persons). In the DNT-based self-catering annex there are 10 beds. Here you require a DNT standard key, which is available from Ålesund and Sunnmøre Turistforening (Tourist Association), who administer the cabin

Standalhytta in winter dress. Photo: Thomas Hisdal

for DNT. The kitchen is well-equipped with a fridge and other kitchen utensils.

Approach: Follow the RV655 from the centre of Ørsta in the direction of Sæbø. At the bridge at Høgebrua, after about 4 km, drive straight ahead for about 7 km towards Kolåsen. From there take the gravel road that is open all winter and continue for roughly 4 km up to where the road reaches its highest point. Standalhytta is the large black cabin high up on the left-hand side.

Prices: Members: NOK 185 pr night. Non-members: NOK 285 pr night. Discounts for children, youths and families.

Telephone: +47 70 06 11 17

Website: www.aast.no

Patchellhytta with Slogen in the background. Photo: Karstein Ringstad

HJØRUNDFJORDEN

PATCHELLHYTTA is administered by Ålesund and Sunnmøre Turistforening (Tourist Association) for DNT. It is a self-catering cabin with 50 beds situated at a height of 800 metres surrounded by the majestic peaks Slogen, Smørskredtindane and Brekketindane. It is possible to purchase dry foodstuffs from the self-service food store at the cabin. The kitchen is well-equipped with kitchen utensils.

Approach: You can reach the cabin from three sides. The easiest, but longest route goes up the Habostaddalen valley from Stranda. The shortest, but without doubt steepest, climbs the slope up from the farms at Skylstad in Norangsdalen. Here we describe the route from Haukåssætra above Urke. Follow the RV655 from Ørsta to Sæbø. Take the ferry Sæbø-Lekneset. Follow the signposts to Urkedalen from the RV655. Park beside the power station above Haukåssætra, or further down the valley if the road is blocked by snow. Follow the marked path north of the water course until you reach the snow. Keep slightly west of the valley bottom of the gentle Langseterdalen. Go up Steinreset and on down to the cabin in Habostaddalen. The trip will take you roughly two hours from the power station.

Prices: Members: NOK 185 pr night. Non-members: NOK 285 pr night. Discounts for children, youths and families.

Telephone: +47 70 06 11 17

Website: www.aast.no

HUSTADNES FJORDHYTTER lie is a beautiful spot down beside the Hjørundfjord, 2 km from the centre of Sæbø, where you will find shops, cafes, bank and post office. The cabins enjoy a high standard with kitchen, bathroom, spacious outdoor area for barbecues and a large outdoor jacuzzi. You can also hire a boat.

Approach: Follow the RV655 from Ørsta to Sæbø. Immediately after the signpost marked Sæbø, turn right across a bridge. Drive past the campsite and turn left at the next junction. At the end of the road you will find Hustadnes Fjordhytter.

Season: Open all year round.

Prices: Off-peak season: 4-bed cabin NOK 350 pr night. 8-bed cabin NOK 900 pr night.

Peak season: 4-bed cabin NOK 550 pr night. 8-bed cabin NOK 1000 pr night.

Address: Hustadnes Fjordhytter, 6165 Sæbø.

Telephone: +47 70 04 00 85

E-mail: mail@hustadnes-fjordhytter.no

Website: www.hustadnes-fjordhytter.no

HOTEL UNION ØYE is perhaps the most venerable and impressive of all the locations offering accommodation in Sunnmøre. This was where the nobility of Europe came to stay and enjoy the scenery of Sunnmøre in the hotel's heyday from 1890-1940. It was also frequently visited by climbing pioneers from the British aristocracy, who used it as a base from which to climb new routes on Slogen, Smørskredtindane, Brekketindane and Råna. During this period Patchell, Slingsby, Arbutnot and Oppenheim performed spectacular first ascents on these now so famous peaks. A large new extension is planned to be opened in the near future, from which time the hotel will remain open all the year round.

Approach: Follow the RV655 from Ørsta to Sæbø. Take the ferry Sæbø-Lekneset, and continue along the RV655 for about 8 km as far as Øye.

Lisje-Standaldalsætra high above the Hjørundfjord. Photo: Håvard Myklebust

Season:	1st May – 31st December.
Prices 2010:	Double room including breakfast from NOK 995 pr person.
Address:	AS Hotel Union Øye, 6196 Norangsfjorden.
Telephone:	+47 70 06 21 00
E-mail:	post@unionoye.no
Website:	www.unionoye.no

VILLA NORANGDAL presents itself today as a stylish boutique hotel with a high standard. In its heyday from 1890-1940 Hotel Norangdal was frequently visited by the royalty and aristocracy of Europe, as well as from a number of British climbing pioneers. Slingsby was particularly interested in Kvitegga (1717m) and in 1900 he made the first ascent of the magnificent north-east ridge of this majestic peak. The hotel closed its doors in 1960, but in 2000 the new owner reopened the hotel after a long period of restoration work. Each room has been tastefully designed and furnished in the style of a different decade: the 1920s, -30s, -40s, -50, -60s and -70s. All the food is made from local Norwegian produce and is excellent, both early in the morning and at dinner in the evening. After a long day in the mountains you can also jump into the jacuzzi and enjoy a cold beer from the local brewery "Slogen". The hotel offers free wireless Internet access, but mobile phone coverage is poor.

Approach:	Follow the RV655 from Ørsta to Sæbø. Take the ferry Sæbø-Lekneset, and continue along the RV655. Drive past Øye and up through the fantastic Norangsdalen. From Øye it is about 13 km to Villa Norangdal, which you will find high up on the right of the road.
Season:	From mid-June to the end of August you may check in without a booking, but the rest of the year a minimum of six persons must book well in advance.
Prices 2010:	Double room including breakfast & packed lunch NOK 990 pr person. NOK 1350 for single room.
Telephone:	+47 70 26 10 84
E-mail:	mail@norangdal.com
Website:	www.norangdal.com

TAFJORDFJELLA, INDRE SUNNMØRE

EIDSDAL

SMOGEHUSET offers overnight accommodation in a building that has really retained its soul. The old wooden house has been restored through a combination of charm and hard work by mine hosts, a Norwegian-Swedish couple who provide excellent service. You really get the feeling of "coming home". You will find it hard to forget a stay at this unique location. The house maintains a high standard with a good kitchen, bathroom and a glass veranda in every room. In Eidsdalen there is a shop, cafe and bank.

Approach:	Follow the RV655 from Ørsta to Sæbø. Take the ferry Sæbø-Lekneset, and continue along the RV655. Drive past Øye and through the fantastic Norangsdalen. Turn left at the T-junction and follow the RV62 to Hellesylt. Take the spectacular ferry trip from Hellesylt to Geiranger. On driving ashore turn left onto the RV63 and make your way up the hairpins of the Ørnesvingane before cruising down the long valley to Eidsdal.
Season:	May - September. Otherwise booking in advance.

Prices 2010:	Off-peak season: NOK 250 pr person. Peak season: NOK 350 pr person. 4-bed cabin: NOK 1000.
Address:	Fam.Blindheim, 6215 Eidsdal
Telephone:	+47 71 49 09 89
E-mail:	smogehuset@hotmail.com

NORDDAL

HERDALSSÆTRA lies right in the heart of the World Heritage area Western Norwegian Landscape. The idyllic Herdalssætra in Norddal has an unbroken 300-year seter tradition and with its 300 milking goats is one of Norway's biggest summer grazing cooperatives. There are also cows, sheep and Norwegian fjord horses on the mountain pastures. The seter hamlet also has a unique architectural environment with over 30 different seter buildings in a cluster. Until the early 1700s the place was permanently occupied, and the farm history stretches back to Viking times. The seter buildings in Herdalen are equipped with bed linen, but guests must bring their own duvet covers. All the necessary kitchen equipment is provided, gas stoves for cooking and wood-burning stoves for heating. The cafe can tempt you with local specialities such as brown goat's cheese, Herdal's own caramel toffees, cured leg of goat, salted and dried ribs of mutton and smoked sausage made of goat's meat flavoured with spices and herbs from the mountains. Herdalssætra is a good starting point for mountain hikes to e.g. Torvløysa (1851m), Heregga (1557m) and Trollknivsegga (1530m).

Approach:	Follow the RV655 from Ørsta to Sæbø. Take the ferry Sæbø-Lekneset, and continue along the RV655. Drive past Øye and through the fantastic Norangsdalen. Turn left at the T-junction and follow the RV62 to Hellesylt. Take the spectacular ferry trip from Hellesylt to Geiranger. On driving ashore turn left onto the RV63 and make your way up the hairpins of the Ørnesvingane before cruising down the long valley to Eidsdal. On the ferry quay at Eidsdal turn right and drive about 4 km to Norddal. From Norddal it is a drive of about 9 km up to Herdalssætra.
Season:	Overnight accommodation can be booked all year round. The cafe is open from mid-June to mid-September.
Prices 2010:	1 hut NOK 600 pr night. NOK 3800 pr week.
Address:	Herdalssætra, 6214 Norddal
Telephone:	+47 70 25 91 08
E-mail:	jossande@online.no setra@herdalssetra.no
Website:	www.herdalssetra.no
Or	
Telephone:	+47 92 28 34 77
E-mail:	petter.melchior@c2i.net
Website:	www.thehappyend.no

VALLDAL

JUVET LANDSKAPSHOTELL is perched on a precipitous river bank between pine and birch trees and large cliffs. What is unique about the hotel is perhaps not the rooms, but the view you get from the windows. The hotel is built ecologically, with a large spa and various sauna alternatives. An outdoor jacuzzi with a huge panorama terrace is also part of the facilities. Breakfast is served in a converted cowshed.

Approach:	Follow the RV655 from Ørsta to Sæbø. Take the ferry Sæbø-Lekneset, and continue along the RV655. Drive past Øye and through the fantastic Norangsdalen. Turn left at the T-junction and follow the RV62 to Hellesylt. Take the spectacular ferry trip from Hellesylt to Geiranger. On driving ashore turn left onto the RV63 and make your way up the hairpins of the Ørnesvingane before cruising down the long valley to Eidsdal. Take the ferry Eidsdal-Linge. Follow the RV63 from the centre of Valldal for about 20 km as far as Gudbrandsbrua. Turn left about 100 metres after the bridge.
Season:	March-December.
Prices:	NOK 1250 pr person in a double room including breakfast.
Telephone:	+47 95 03 20 10
E-mail:	knut@juvet.com
Website:	www.juvet.com

The stunning view from Juvet landskapshotell. Photo: Knut Slinning

GEIRANGER

GRANDE HYTTEUTLEIGE OG CAMPING is beautifully situated right on the edge of the Geiranger-fjord, 2 km from the village centre. You can rent cabins of various sizes and standard. Boats are also available for hire.

Approach:	From Oslo/Trondheim you take the E6 to Otta. Here you turn off onto the RV15 passing Lom on the way towards Stryn. Drive a few kilometres past the mountain hotel at Grotli on Strynefjell and then turn right onto the RV63 towards Geiranger. From Ørsta you take the RV655 to Sæbø. Cross on the ferry from Sæbø – Lekneset and continue through the Norangdalen valley until you reach the RV60, where you turn left and head down to Hellesylt. Take the ferry up the Geirangerfjord, and turn left on disembarking. Drive out along the fjord for 2 km past Ørnevegen to the campsite down by the water's edge.
Season:	May - October. The cabin can also be rented off season.
Prices:	Off-peak season: smallest cabin NOK 410 pr night. Largest cabin NOK 870 pr night.
Peak season:	smallest cabin NOK 510 pr night. Largest cabin NOK 1090 pr night.
Address:	Grande hytteutleige og camping, Grande, 6216 Geiranger
Telephone:	+47 70 26 30 68
E-mail:	office@grande-hytteutleige.no
Website:	www.grande-hytteutleige.no

Grande Hytteutleige & Camping on the shores of the Geirangerfjord. Photo: Eirik Vaage

MARINAS FOR VISITORS

There are a number of good marinas around Sunnmøre that welcome visitors with large or small craft. For more detailed information we refer you to www.gjestehavner.no

18.3 TOURIST INFORMATION OFFICES

ULSTEINVIK

Turistinformasjonen i Ulsteinvik

Address:	Sjøgata 63, 6065 Ulsteinvik
Telephone:	+47 70 01 75 10
E-mail:	turistinformasjonen@ulstein. kommune.no
Website:	www.ulstein.kommune.no

ÅLESUND

Turistinformasjonen i Ålesund

Address:	Skateflukaia, 6002 Ålesund
Telephone:	+47 70 15 76 00
E-mail:	info@visitalesund.com
Website:	www.visitalesund-geiranger. com

ØRSTA

Turistinformasjonen i Ørsta

Address:	Parkvegen 7, 6150 Ørsta
Telephone:	+47 70 06 85 18
E-mail:	info@orstainfo.no
Website:	www.orstainfo.no

GEIRANGER

Destination Geirangerfjord Trollstigen

Address:	6216 Geiranger
Telephone:	+47 70 26 38 00
E-mail:	info@visitgeirangerfjorden. com
Website:	www.visitalesund-geiranger. com

SYKKYLVEN

Sykkylven Reiselivsforum

Address:	c/o Norsk Møbelfaglig senter Postboks 288, 6239 Sykkylven
Telephone:	+47 70 25 30 03
E-mail:	post@sykkylven.net
Website:	www.sykkylven.net

STORDALEN

Stordal Turistinformasjon

Address:	Sentrum, 6250 Stordal
Telephone:	+47 90 36 13 48
E-mail:	post@visitstordal.no
Website:	www.visitstordal.no

Camping, cooking and climbing in Øvstefeltet above the Austefjord. Photo: Knut Arne Aarset

19 LITERATURE, WEBSITES, COMPETITIONS AND FESTIVALS

19.1 LITERATURE

MOUNTAINS AND CLIMBING

Skiturar i Sunnmørsalpane – Fjella vest for Hjørundfjorden, 1996. Here you will find photos and descriptions of 80 ski trips in the western reaches of the Sunnmøre Alps. The first edition was sold out long ago, but it is possible a new skiing book will be published in the not too distant future. Until then, you can find some descriptions at www.iriss.no

Fotturar på Sunnmøre (4.edition 2010). Here you will find photos and descriptions of the vast majority of the hiking trips in the Sunnmøre Alps as a whole. You will also find some descriptions at www.iriss.no

Molladalen (1989). Here there are photos and descriptions of 60 climbing routes in Molladalen. This old climbing guidebook from 1989 was sold out long ago, but the publishers are planning a new book. Until then, you can find descriptions of a number of routes at www.iriss.no

Stiguide til indre Storfjorden – Fjørå singletrack camp by Håvard Melbø, 2009. Here you will find photos and descriptions of a series of great steep cycling routes in the mountains of Inner Storfjord.

Klippeklatring og buldring på Sunnmøre, by Tommy Skeide. Here you will find photos and descriptions from a number of different crags and bouldering fields in Sunnmøre. The guidebook will probably be published in 2012.

From the X2 festival at Bondalseidet. Photo: Karl Otto Kristiansen

19.2 WEBSITES

ADVENTURE CENTRES

www.actin.no
www.valldal.no
www.sykkylven-aktiv.no
www.ullahavsportsenter.no

CROSS-COUNTRY/MOUNTAIN BIKING

www.fjellstova.no
www.kragebakk.no

MOUNTAINS AND CLIMBING

www.iriss.no
www.skk-nytt.com
www.klivrelaget.com
www.klatreklubben.no
www.klatre.com

PARAGLIDING

www.himmelseglarane.com
www.aapgk.net

SCUBA DIVING

www.heroy-dykkerklubb.com
www.aegir.no
www.dykkersenter.no

SURFING

www.stadsurfing.com
www.lapoint.no

VIKING LONGSHIPS

www.helset.net

ÅLESUND AND SUNNMØRE TOURIST ASSOCIATION

www.aast.no

19.3 COMPETITIONS AND FESTIVALS

X2 is one of Norway's most enjoyable skiing and extreme sport festivals. For more info: www.x2ski.no

ALPERITTET is a long and demanding skiing competition. It involves running off-piste from Roalds-hornet all the way down to the town centre in Stranda. For more info: www.alperittet.com

STANDALRENNET is a skiing competition at Standalhytta with traditions dating back to as early as 1909. For more info: www.aask.no

SAUDEHORNET rett opp is one of Norway's steepest fell running competitions in the summer. For more info: www.saudehornet.no

SOMMARFESTIVALEN is a hippie party on the island of Giske outside Ålesund with international artists where you pay a voluntary donation to get in. For more info: www.verdensbestefestival.no

DOKUMENTARFILMFESTIVALEN in Volda has earned itself a reputation both nationally and internationally as an excellent documentary film festival. More info at www.dokfilm.no

MATFESTIVALEN is a grand celebration of food and drink in the city centre in Ålesund, where sea-food in particular is the main focus. More info at www.matfestivalen.no

HERØYSPELET is an open-air theatre performance with its roots in local history, played out on the island of Herøy with the open sea as a backdrop. More info at www.heroyspelet.no

ÅLESUND BÅTFESTIVAL is a large gathering of all manner of craft and boats, which also attracts huge numbers of people to the city centre in Ålesund. More info at www.batfestivalen.no

Acrobatics during the Boat Festival in the centre of Ålesund.
Photo: Arnfinn Tønnesen

Full moon over Romedalen. Photo: Arnfinn Tønnesen.

THANKS FOR COMING ALONG

We, the authors, would like in this way to thank everyone who has been so helpful and patient during the realisation of this rather complex book project. It has been a long and winding road for us novices in the world of publishing, and without the help and support of so many people, we would not have made it to the end of the road. First of all we would like to thank Alvaro Susena, who gave us really useful strategic tips and advice, especially during the initial phase of the project. Then we must express our gratitude to all those who have supplied us with texts and descriptions of routes for those activities that we ourselves are not experts at. In particular we have in mind Joar Wæhle, who helped us with the chapters on river paddling and mountain biking, Tommy Skeide, who helped us draw up guides for the cliff climbing and bouldering fields that are presented and Lill Haugen, who was generous enough to provide us with both text and photos for the chapter on scuba diving. We would also like to mention the assistance given by the widely experienced author of many tour guidebooks Helge J. Standal, who among other things placed his rich archive of photographs at our disposal. Our thanks are also due to all those who provided us with first-class action photos, all of whom have been acknowledged in the captions accompanying the photos. We would never have been able to produce a product of this quality without these photographs, since it is virtually impossible to cover such a wide range of activities and localities with our own photos. In addition we would like to express our gratitude to those who were kind enough to act as photo models on our many trips and activities. Thanks also to our publishers Fri Flyt, and especially to Erlend Sande and Eva Camilla Brandt, for their incredible desire and ability to fulfil our wishes and intentions in writing this book.

Last, but by no means least, we must say a big thank you to our ever-patient partners who have put up with us over the last two years: Sigrid, Vibeke and Clara.

With best wishes from the authors

STIG J. HELSET from Ørsta now lives in Volda. He has completed all the ski trips and hikes that are presented and climbed most of the routes that are described here and thus written the texts and drawn the sketches in connection with these activities. Stig has also had the overall responsibility for editing the texts and routes in the book. When he is not up a mountain somewhere, he works as Associate Professor in Norwegian at Volda University College.

FREDRIK SIGURDH is a Swede who now lives in Ålesund. He came up with the idea of this book and has made important contributions to several chapters. He now works as a catering manager at an offshore oil installation in the North Sea. Tourism development in Sunnmøre is a passion of his and he has initiated a research project in cooperation with Møreforskning on the topic. Moreover, he is in the process of building up Creare Innovare, a company that specializes in project design.

EIRIK VAAGE from Volda has had the main responsibility for the photographs in the book. He himself has taken many of the best action shots and also the majority of the aerial photographs. In addition he has put in a huge effort in collecting, categorising and editing the photographs from other photographers. Eirik has also written the texts on longboarding and surfing. He is joint owner and part of the team running the media house Frost Media.

Topping out on Grøtdalstindane. Kolåstinden in the background. Photo: Christopher Woldsund

Legend

- ● Alpine ski touring
- ✕ Ski areas
- | Ice climbing
- — Hiking
- ● Mountain climbing
- ✕ Sports climbing/bouldering
- | Scenic bike routes
- — Mountain biking
- ● Paragliding
- ✕ Scuba diving
- | Sea and fjord paddling
- ▨ Kayaking
- ● Longboarding
- ✕ Windsurfing and kiting
- | Surfing

Storholmen fyr

Ulla fyr
347

490

22 Roald

Erkna fyr

Nordstran

Giske

ALESUND

Brandal

Flø

Hareid

Ulsteinvik

Vartdal

977

Leine

654

Haddal

1045

Liadal

Ørsta

Kvalsvik

Kvalsund

332

655

Svinøy

431

592

Bringsing haug

652

61

Aram

Volda

497

Dalsfjord

651

Kjerringa

Fiskå

540

1097

842

Leikanger

Syvden

Blæja

Trollvass tinden

645

1332

Skongenes

Selje

Kråkenes

620

Anelfoten

504

545

774

1205

1114

1002

Haddeberg

951

983

330

787

E k

Bryggja

618

Stårheim

Nordfjordeid

380

Oldeide

549

Rugsund

616

719

Lote

681

889

Leirgulen

Bremanger

614

Sandane